CIVIL PROCEDURE THROUGH CASES

Law in Pieces Series

Anjanette G. Seymour, LL.M., LL.B. (Hons.)

This work is published as part of 'Law in Pieces' series of study snippets. It is intended as an educational aid, blending narrative and doctrinal explanation, and should not be construed as a full textbook or novel. The content herein does not constitute legal advice. Readers should consult authoritative sources and law professors for comprehensive guidance. This volume contains a curated selection of Civil Procedure cases.

Cover Design: Anjanette G. Seymour

ISBN:9798995892380

TABLE OF CONTENTS

Part I. Personal Jurisdiction

Part II. Subject Matter Jurisdiction

Supplemental Subject Matter Jurisdiction Cases

Part III. Venue & Transfer

Hoffman v. Blaski (1960)

Part IV. Erie Doctrine

Gasperini v. Center for Humanities (1996)

Hanna v. Plumer (1965)

Byrd v. Blue Ridge Rural Electric Cooperative (1958)

Guaranty Trust Co. v. York (1945)

Erie Railroad Co. v. Tompkins (1938)

Swift v. Tyson (1842)

Part V. Pleading

Ashcroft v. Iqbal (2009)

Bell Atlantic Corp. v. Twombly (2007)

Conley v. Gibson (1957)

Part VI. Summary Judgment

Celotex Corp. v. Catrett (1986)

Anderson v. Liberty Lobby, Inc. (1986)

Matsushita Electric Industrial Co. v. Zenith Radio Corp. (1986)

Part VII. Discovery

Upjohn Co. v. United States (1981)

Hickman v. Taylor (1947)

Part VII. Claim Preclusion

Part IX. Issue Preclusion

Part X. Supplemental Jurisdiction

Part XI. Joinder

PREFACE — *LAW IN PIECES*

The *Law in Pieces* series was created with a single purpose: to transform legal education through narrative clarity.

Each volume breaks doctrine into stories, patterns, and principles. Each case is retold with emotional clarity and doctrinal precision. Each chapter is designed to spark the moment every student deserves — the moment when the law finally "clicks" the "aha" moments.

Across the series, you will find:

-Narrative case retellings that illuminate doctrine

-Clean doctrinal rules distilled from complex opinions

-Visual and structural clarity

-A focus on epiphany, not memorization

-A commitment to accessibility without sacrificing rigor

Law in Pieces is more than a study aid. It is a pedagogical philosophy — one that honors the humanity behind the law and the students who work so hard to master it.

Whether you are reading your first volume or you have read others in the series, I hope this series becomes a trusted companion on your journey through law school and beyond.

AUTHOR'S NOTE

Law school is often described as a rite of passage — a journey through dense doctrine, unfamiliar language, and the quiet pressure to "think like a lawyer." I remember that journey well. I remember the moments of clarity, the moments of confusion, and the moments when a single case suddenly made everything make sense.

This book was born from those moments.

Civil Procedure Through Cases is part of a larger vision: to make legal doctrine accessible, human, and memorable. Every case in this book was chosen not only for its doctrinal importance, but for the story it tells — a story about conflict, strategy, fairness, and the architecture of justice.

My hope is simple: That these narratives help you see the law not as a maze, but as a map. That you feel grounded, not overwhelmed. That you find clarity where others found confusion. And that you carry these stories with you into your exams and doing assignments.

Thank you for allowing my work to be part of your learning journey. May it bring you confidence, insight, and a sense of connection to the long tradition of lawyers who learned the law one case at a time.

— Anjanette G. Seymour, LL.M., LL.B. (Hons.)

INTRODUCTION

Civil Procedure Through Cases is built on the belief that doctrine becomes unforgettable when it is anchored in narrative. Each case is retold with clarity and emotional resonance, revealing not only what the court held, but *why* the dispute mattered, *how* the conflict unfolded, and *what* the decision teaches about the structure of our legal system.

You will not find sterile summaries here. You will find stories — stories that illuminate jurisdiction, discovery, joinder, preclusion, and the strategic choreography of litigation. Stories that show how ordinary people, corporations, unions, and governments collided in ways that shaped the rules.

This book is designed to give you:

> **Clarity** when doctrine feels overwhelming
>
> **Confidence** when cases seem dense or technical
>
> **Connection** to the human stakes behind procedural rules
>
> **A narrative map** that ties the entire course together

Civil Procedure is not just a set of rules. It is a story about power, fairness, and the structure of justice. This book invites you to learn that story — one case at a time.

Personal Jurisdiction Cases

Personal Jurisdiction determines **whether a court has the power to require a particular defendant to appear and defend a lawsuit**. Unlike subject matter jurisdiction, which focuses on the court's authority, personal jurisdiction is about **fairness to the defendant** and the defendant's connection to the forum state.

The core idea is simple: **A defendant should not be sued in a place where they have no meaningful ties.**

Personal jurisdiction comes in two main forms:

> **General Jurisdiction** — the defendant's contacts with the state are so continuous and systematic that they can be sued there for *any* claim, even unrelated ones.
>
> **Specific Jurisdiction** — the lawsuit arises out of or relates to the defendant's contacts with the state, and exercising jurisdiction is fair and reasonable.

Courts look for **minimum contacts, purposeful availment**, and **foreseeability** — asking whether the defendant reached into the state, benefited from it, or should reasonably expect to be sued there.

Examples

Example 1: General Jurisdiction (Allowed)

A corporation is incorporated in Delaware and has its headquarters in California. It can be sued in **either** place for **any** claim, even if the events happened elsewhere. These are its "home" states.

Example 2: Specific Jurisdiction (Allowed)

A Florida company ships a defective product to a customer in Wisconsin. The product injures the customer in Wisconsin. Because the company **purposefully sent** the product into the state and the injury happened there, Wisconsin courts may hear the case.

Example 3: No Purposeful Availment (Not Allowed)

A New York driver gets into an accident in New York with a Wisconsin resident. The Wisconsin resident later tries to sue the driver in Wisconsin. The New York driver has **no contacts** with Wisconsin, so Wisconsin courts cannot exercise jurisdiction.

Example 4: Internet Contacts (Depends)

A website accessible everywhere does **not** automatically create jurisdiction everywhere. But if the business **targets** customers in a specific state — advertising, shipping, or interacting with residents — that may create specific jurisdiction.

Summary

Personal jurisdiction asks whether it is fair and constitutional to require this defendant to defend this lawsuit in this state.

Ford Motor Co. v. Montana Eighth Judicial District Court (2021)

Narrative Facts

Two separate accidents occurred in Montana and Minnesota involving Ford vehicles — one a malfunctioning tire, the other an airbag failure. The injured plaintiffs sued Ford in their home states. Ford pushed back, arguing that because the specific cars involved were not originally sold, designed, or manufactured in those states, the courts lacked personal jurisdiction. Ford insisted that only a strict causal link — "the car must have entered the state because of us" — could justify jurisdiction. But the plaintiffs argued that Ford had spent years cultivating a market in both states: advertising, selling, servicing, and maintaining a strong commercial presence. The question became whether a company that deliberately serves a state's market can avoid being sued there simply because the particular product at issue arrived through a different path.

Issue

Whether a state court may exercise specific personal jurisdiction over a defendant when the defendant extensively serves the state's market for the product at issue, even if the particular item involved in the accident was not sold or designed there.

Holding

Yes. A state may exercise specific jurisdiction when the defendant has purposefully cultivated the state's market for the very product involved in the litigation, even without a strict causal link.

Reasoning

1. **Purposeful Availment Exists.** Ford deliberately marketed, sold, and serviced the same models of vehicles in both states, creating a substantial connection with the forum.
2. **"Arise Out Of or Relate To" Is Broader Than Strict Causation.** The Court emphasized that "relate to" allows jurisdiction when the defendant's forum activities are closely connected to the type of product and harm at issue.
3. **Fairness and Predictability.** Ford could reasonably anticipate being sued in states where it actively promotes and supports its vehicles.
4. **State Interest.** States have a strong interest in providing a forum for residents injured by products widely sold and supported within their borders.

Final Takeaway

Ford confirms that **specific jurisdiction does not require a perfect causal chain**. If a company **deliberately serves a state's market**, and the lawsuit concerns the **same type of product**, the connection is strong enough. Think of it as a web: if the defendant has woven itself into the commercial life of the state, it cannot pretend the strands don't exist when litigation arises.

Bristol-Myers Squibb Co. v. Superior Court (2017)

Narrative Facts

Bristol-Myers Squibb (BMS) sold a popular blood-thinning drug, Plavix, nationwide. Hundreds of plaintiffs sued the company in California state court, claiming the drug caused serious injuries. But most of those plaintiffs did **not** live in California, nor had they bought or taken the drug there. Their claims had no direct tie to the state. BMS did have a strong commercial presence in California — research facilities, sales operations, and marketing — but none of those activities were connected to the out-of-state plaintiffs' injuries. The question became whether a company's broad national footprint allows plaintiffs from anywhere to sue in a state where the defendant does business, even if the claims themselves have no connection to that state.

Issue

Whether a state court may exercise specific personal jurisdiction over claims brought by non-resident plaintiffs when those claims have no connection to the defendant's activities in the forum state.

Holding

No. Specific jurisdiction requires a connection between the forum state and the particular claims at issue; general business activity in the state is not enough.

Reasoning

1. **Claim-Specific Connection Required.** The Court emphasized that each plaintiff's claim must "arise

out of or relate to" the defendant's contacts with the forum. The non-resident plaintiffs could not show this link.

2. **General Presence Is Not Specific Jurisdiction.** Even though BMS had extensive operations in California, those activities were unrelated to the injuries of the out-of-state plaintiffs.

3. **No Sliding Scale.** California's attempt to use a "more contacts = less connection needed" approach was rejected. The Court held that due process does not allow a relaxed standard.

4. **Fairness and Predictability.** Allowing states to hear claims with no forum connection would undermine the territorial limits of judicial power and create unpredictability for defendants.

Final Takeaway

Bristol-Myers draws a bright line: **specific jurisdiction is claim-specific**. A defendant's general business footprint in a state does not open the door to lawsuits from plaintiffs whose claims have **no tie** to that state. Think of it as a lock-and-key rule — the forum contact must fit the claim, not just the company.

Daimler AG v. Bauman (2014)

Narrative Facts

A group of Argentinian plaintiffs sued Daimler in California, alleging that one of Daimler's subsidiaries in Argentina had collaborated with the military dictatorship to commit human rights abuses decades earlier. The plaintiffs chose California because Daimler's U.S. subsidiary, Mercedes-Benz USA, had a strong commercial presence there: dealerships, advertising, and significant sales. But the alleged wrongdoing had nothing to do with California, and the plaintiffs were not California residents. The question became whether a multinational corporation could be sued in a state simply because it does a lot of business there, even when the claims have no connection to that state.

Issue

Whether a state may exercise general personal jurisdiction over a foreign corporation based solely on the substantial business activities of its subsidiary within the forum state.

Holding

No. A corporation is subject to general jurisdiction only where it is "at home," typically its place of incorporation or principal place of business; extensive sales or operations in a state do not make it "at home" there.

Reasoning

1. **General Jurisdiction Is Narrow.** The Court emphasized that general jurisdiction is reserved for places where the corporation is truly "at home," not everywhere it does significant business.

2. **Subsidiary Contacts Do Not Automatically Transfer.** The activities of Mercedes-Benz USA in California could not be imputed to Daimler for general jurisdiction purposes.

3. **Predictability and Fairness.** Allowing general jurisdiction wherever a company has large sales would expose global corporations to suit in virtually every state, undermining due process.

4. **Exceptional Cases Are Rare.** The Court noted that only in extraordinary circumstances would a corporation be "at home" outside its incorporation or headquarters.

Final Takeaway

Daimler dramatically limits general jurisdiction. A corporation is "at home" in only a few places, and **doing a lot of business in a state is not enough**. Think of general jurisdiction as a company's legal home address — not every place it visits, sells, or advertises.

Goodyear Dunlop Tires Operations, S.A. v. Brown (2011)

Narrative Facts

Two young boys from North Carolina were killed in a bus accident overseas. Their parents believed the accident was caused by a defective tire manufactured by Goodyear's foreign subsidiaries. The families sued in North Carolina, even though the tires involved were made and sold entirely abroad. Goodyear's foreign subsidiaries did not design, manufacture, or sell those tires in North Carolina. Only a small number of unrelated Goodyear tires reached the state through the "stream of commerce." The question became whether a foreign corporation could be sued in a state simply because some of its products, unrelated to the lawsuit, ended up there.

Issue

Whether a state may exercise general personal jurisdiction over foreign subsidiaries when their products reach the forum state only through limited, sporadic sales unrelated to the claims.

Holding

No. Sporadic or isolated product flow into a state does not make a foreign corporation "at home" there for purposes of general jurisdiction.

Reasoning

1. **General Jurisdiction Requires Being "At Home."** The Court reaffirmed that general jurisdiction applies only where the corporation's

affiliations are so continuous and systematic that it is essentially at home in the forum.

2. **Limited Product Flow Is Not Enough.** A small number of tires entering North Carolina through the stream of commerce did not create the deep ties needed for general jurisdiction.

3. **No Connection to the Claims.** The specific tires involved in the accident were never sold or distributed in North Carolina, further weakening any jurisdictional basis.

4. **Due Process Limits.** Allowing general jurisdiction based on minimal, unrelated sales would stretch due process beyond its constitutional boundaries.

Final Takeaway

Goodyear draws a firm boundary: **general jurisdiction is rare and requires deep roots**, not scattered or accidental product presence. A corporation is not "at home" in a state simply because some of its goods happen to arrive there. Think of general jurisdiction as a company's permanent residence, not a place it occasionally visits.

J. McIntyre Machinery, Ltd. v. Nicastro (2011)

Narrative Facts

A scrap-metal worker in New Jersey severely injured his hand while using a metal-shearing machine manufactured by a British company, J. McIntyre Machinery. The machine reached the United States through an independent distributor, not through any direct effort by the manufacturer to target New Jersey specifically. The company had attended trade shows in the U.S. and hoped to sell machines nationwide, but it had no offices, employees, or advertising directed at New Jersey. The injured worker sued in New Jersey state court, arguing that by seeking access to the U.S. market generally, the company should expect to be sued wherever its products caused harm. The manufacturer countered that it never targeted New Jersey and therefore could not be forced to defend a lawsuit there.

Issue

Whether a state may exercise specific personal jurisdiction over a foreign manufacturer whose product reaches the forum through the stream of commerce when the manufacturer did not purposefully target that specific state.

Holding

No. A defendant must purposefully target the forum state itself; targeting the U.S. market as a whole is not enough to establish specific jurisdiction.

Reasoning

1. **Purposeful Availment Must Be State-Specific.** The Court emphasized that due process requires the defendant to deliberately engage with the forum state, not merely hope to reach the national market.

2. **Stream of Commerce Alone Is Insufficient.** The machine's arrival in New Jersey through a distributor did not show that the manufacturer directed its conduct toward New Jersey.

3. **Sovereignty and Predictability.** States may exercise jurisdiction only when the defendant's actions connect it to that particular state, preserving predictable limits on judicial power.

4. **Plurality Opinion.** The fractured decision left the doctrine unsettled, but the controlling principle is that **general U.S. targeting is not enough**.

Final Takeaway

Nicastro narrows the stream-of-commerce theory: **a defendant must intentionally reach into the specific state**, not just the national market. Think of it as a spotlight — the defendant must shine its light on the forum, not merely glow in the background of the U.S. market.

Asahi Metal Industry Co. v. Superior Court (1987)

Narrative Facts

A California motorcyclist was seriously injured when a tire on his bike suddenly blew out. He sued the Taiwanese company that made the tire tube. That company, in turn, filed a cross-claim against Asahi Metal Industry, a Japanese manufacturer of the valve assemblies used in the tube. The original plaintiff eventually settled, leaving only the dispute between two foreign companies. Asahi argued that California had no business pulling a Japanese company into court when the accident happened in California, but Asahi itself had never advertised, sold, or targeted the California market. Its products reached the state only because the Taiwanese company incorporated Asahi's valves into finished tubes sold worldwide. The question became whether merely placing a component into the stream of commerce — knowing it might end up anywhere — was enough to justify personal jurisdiction in a specific state.

Issue

Whether a state may exercise specific personal jurisdiction over a foreign component manufacturer whose product enters the forum state only through the stream of commerce, without the manufacturer purposefully directing its conduct toward that state.

Holding

No. The Court held that California's exercise of jurisdiction over Asahi would violate due process because Asahi did not purposefully target California, and the exercise of jurisdiction would be unreasonable.

Reasoning

1. **No Purposeful Direction Toward the Forum.** The Justices agreed that Asahi did not deliberately target California; its components reached the state only because another company sold finished products there.

2. **Stream of Commerce Debate.** The Court split on whether mere awareness that products may reach a state is enough. Some Justices required additional conduct (advertising, designing for the market), while others believed awareness alone could suffice.

3. **Unreasonableness of Jurisdiction.** All Justices agreed that exercising jurisdiction over a Japanese company in a dispute between two foreign entities placed an undue burden on Asahi and served minimal state interests.

4. **International Fairness Concerns.** The Court emphasized the need for caution when asserting jurisdiction over foreign defendants, especially when the forum's interest is weak.

Final Takeaway

Asahi is the cautionary tale of personal jurisdiction: **stream of commerce alone is not enough**, and courts must consider fairness, burden, and the forum's interest. Think of it as a two-step test — even if contacts exist, jurisdiction must still be reasonable. When the forum's stake is thin and the defendant's burden is heavy, due process steps in to say, "not here."

Burger King Corp. v. Rudzewicz (1985)

Narrative Facts

Two Michigan businessmen entered into a long-term franchise agreement with Burger King. The contract required them to follow Burger King's detailed operational standards and to make monthly payments to the company's headquarters in Florida. When the franchisees fell behind on payments, Burger King terminated the franchise. The franchisees refused to leave the restaurant location, and Burger King sued them in Florida. The defendants argued that they had never set foot in Florida and that all their business activities occurred in Michigan. Burger King countered that the defendants had deliberately formed a substantial, ongoing relationship with the Florida headquarters. The question became whether a defendant who enters a long-term, interstate contractual relationship can be sued in the other party's home state even without physical presence.

Issue

Whether a defendant who enters a substantial, ongoing contractual relationship with a forum-state corporation has purposefully established minimum contacts sufficient for specific personal jurisdiction, even without physical presence in the forum.

Holding

Yes. A defendant who deliberately creates a long-term, interstate relationship with a forum-state corporation purposefully avails themselves of that forum, making jurisdiction proper.

Reasoning

1. **Purposeful Availment Through Contractual Relationship.** The franchise agreement created a continuous, structured relationship with Burger King's Florida headquarters, including payments, supervision, and dispute resolution provisions.
2. **Physical Presence Not Required.** The Court emphasized that modern commerce does not require physical entry into a state to establish minimum contacts.
3. **Foreseeability of Being Sued in the Forum.** By entering a heavily regulated, long-term franchise relationship centered in Florida, the defendants could reasonably anticipate litigation there.
4. **Fairness Factors.** Florida had a strong interest in enforcing contracts involving its corporations, and the burden on the defendants was not so severe as to make jurisdiction unreasonable.

Final Takeaway

Burger King teaches that **contracts can create jurisdiction**. When a defendant forms a deliberate, ongoing relationship with a forum-state entity, they are purposefully availing themselves of that state's legal protections and obligations. Think of it as a tether — once you tie yourself to a forum through a structured, long-term agreement, you cannot pretend the connection doesn't exist when disputes arise.

World-Wide Volkswagen Corp. v. Woodson (1980)

Narrative Facts

A New York family bought an Audi from a local dealership and later moved across the country. While driving through Oklahoma, another car struck them, and the Audi caught fire, causing severe injuries. The family sued several defendants in Oklahoma, including the New York retailer and the regional distributor. Those defendants had never advertised in Oklahoma, never shipped cars there, never sold cars there, and had no offices or employees in the state. Their entire business was confined to New York, New Jersey, and Connecticut. The plaintiffs argued that because cars are mobile and often travel across state lines, the defendants should expect to be sued wherever their products cause harm. The defendants countered that they had no purposeful connection to Oklahoma and could not be forced to defend a lawsuit there.

Issue

Whether a state may exercise specific personal jurisdiction over a retailer and distributor whose only connection to the forum is that their product happened to be brought there by a consumer.

Holding

No. A defendant is not subject to personal jurisdiction merely because it is foreseeable that its product might travel to the forum state; the defendant must purposefully direct its activities toward that state.

Reasoning

1. **Foreseeability Alone Is Not Enough.** The Court distinguished between foreseeability that a product may end up in a state and foreseeability of being haled into court there. Only the latter matters for due process.

2. **Purposeful Availment Required.** The defendants had no deliberate contacts with Oklahoma — no sales, no advertising, no distribution channels, no targeting of the state.

3. **Consumer's Unilateral Action Cannot Create Jurisdiction.** The family's decision to drive through Oklahoma did not establish any connection between the defendants and the state.

4. **Predictability and Fair Warning.** Jurisdiction must be based on the defendant's own choices, not on the random movement of products or customers.

Final Takeaway

World-Wide Volkswagen is the backbone of modern personal jurisdiction: **the defendant must reach into the forum; the forum cannot reach out to the defendant**. A product's mobility does not create jurisdiction. Think of it as a rule of intentionality — only the defendant's purposeful actions can open the door to a state's courts.

International Shoe Co. v. Washington (1945)

Narrative Facts

International Shoe was a Delaware corporation with its main offices in Missouri. It employed salesmen who lived and worked in Washington State, taking orders and promoting the company's products. The salesmen did not have authority to finalize contracts, but they regularly solicited business, displayed samples, and sent orders back to Missouri for approval. Washington sought to collect unemployment taxes from the company, arguing that International Shoe was doing business in the state. The company resisted, claiming it had no offices, no warehouses, and no formal presence in Washington. The question became whether a company with ongoing, systematic activities in a state — but no physical headquarters — could be required to answer to that state's courts.

Issue

Whether a state may exercise personal jurisdiction over a corporation whose activities within the forum are continuous and systematic, even if the corporation lacks a physical presence there.

Holding

Yes. A state may exercise jurisdiction when the defendant has "minimum contacts" with the forum such that maintaining the suit does not offend traditional notions of fair play and substantial justice.

Reasoning

1. **Minimum Contacts Standard.** The Court introduced the modern test: jurisdiction is proper when the defendant's contacts with the forum are substantial enough to justify being sued there.

2. **Continuous and Systematic Activities.** International Shoe's sales force created an ongoing commercial presence in Washington, generating significant business for the company.

3. **Fairness and Reciprocity.** By enjoying the benefits and protections of Washington's market, the company could reasonably be required to answer legal obligations there.

4. **Flexibility Over Formalism.** The Court rejected rigid territorial rules and embraced a more practical, fairness-based approach to jurisdiction.

Final Takeaway

International Shoe is the foundation of modern personal jurisdiction. It replaces strict territorial rules with a flexible fairness test: **if a defendant's contacts with the forum are meaningful and deliberate, jurisdiction is proper**. Think of it as the birth of the "minimum contacts" era — a shift from geography to fairness.

Pennoyer v. Neff (1877)

Narrative Facts

Marcus Neff hired an Oregon lawyer, Sylvester Pennoyer, for legal services but never paid the bill. Pennoyer sued Neff in Oregon state court. At the time, Neff was not living in Oregon, and he was never personally served with the lawsuit. Instead, the court allowed service by publication — a notice printed in a local newspaper. When Neff failed to appear, the court entered a default judgment. To satisfy the judgment, Pennoyer seized Neff's Oregon land and sold it. Later, Neff returned, discovered what had happened, and sued to recover his property. He argued that the original judgment was invalid because the court never obtained personal jurisdiction over him. The dispute forced the Supreme Court to confront a fundamental question: how far does a state's power reach when the defendant is not physically present?

Issue

Whether a state court may exercise personal jurisdiction over a non-resident defendant who was not personally served within the state and had no property attached at the start of the lawsuit.

Holding

No. A state court lacks personal jurisdiction over a non-resident defendant unless the defendant is personally served within the state or the defendant's property located in the state is attached at the outset of the suit.

Reasoning

1. **Territorial Limits on State Power.** The Court held that each state's authority is strictly territorial — it cannot reach beyond its borders to bind non-residents.

2. **Personal Service Required.** For in-personam jurisdiction, the defendant must be personally served while physically present in the forum.

3. **Property Attachment Rule.** A state may exercise jurisdiction over property within its borders, but only if the property is attached at the beginning of the lawsuit.

4. **Due Process Concerns.** Service by publication alone was insufficient to satisfy due process for a non-resident with no meaningful connection to the state.

Final Takeaway

Pennoyer represents the old world of personal jurisdiction — a rigid, territorial model where **physical presence** or **attached property** was everything. Think of it as the "fences and borders" era. Although later cases like *International Shoe* transformed the doctrine, Pennoyer remains the starting point for understanding how far we've come.

ADDITIONAL PERSONAL JURISDICTION CASES

These cases deepen and refine the doctrine surrounding specific and general jurisdiction. They are not always required reading in every Civil Procedure course, but they are essential for understanding the nuances of purposeful availment, effects-based jurisdiction, and the evolution from *Pennoyer* to *International Shoe* and beyond.

The additional cases included here are:

-Burnham v. Superior Court (1990) — Tag jurisdiction

-Calder v. Jones (1984) — The effects test

-Keeton v. Hustler Magazine (1984) — Nationwide circulation and forum choice

-Shaffer v. Heitner (1977) — Quasi in rem jurisdiction after *International Shoe*

.

Burnham v. Superior Court (1990)

Narrative Facts

Dennis Burnham, a New Jersey resident, traveled to California on a short business trip and to visit his children. While he was in the state, his estranged wife served him with divorce papers. Burnham argued that California courts could not exercise personal jurisdiction over him because he had no ongoing ties to the state and was only there temporarily. California relied on the long-standing tradition that physical presence in the forum — even momentary — allows a court to assert jurisdiction. The question became whether this traditional "tag jurisdiction" survived the modern minimum-contacts framework established by *International Shoe.*

Issue

Whether a state may exercise personal jurisdiction over a non-resident defendant who is personally served while physically present in the forum, even if the defendant lacks other contacts with the state.

Holding

Yes. Personal service on a defendant while physically present in the forum is sufficient to establish personal jurisdiction.

Reasoning

1. **Historical Tradition.** The Court emphasized that tag jurisdiction has deep roots in American legal history and has always been considered constitutionally valid.

2. **Physical Presence as a Contact.** Even brief presence in the forum creates a meaningful connection that satisfies due process.

3. **Fairness and Notice.** Being served while physically present ensures the defendant receives notice and can anticipate the possibility of litigation.

4. **Plurality but Strong Consensus.** Although the Justices differed in their reasoning, they agreed that tag jurisdiction remains constitutional.

Final Takeaway

Burnham preserves a simple, bright-line rule: **if you are physically in the state and served with process, the court has jurisdiction over you**. Think of it as the one part of *Pennoyer* that survived untouched — presence still matters.

Calder v. Jones (1984)

Narrative Facts

Shirley Jones, a well-known entertainer living and working in California, sued the National Enquirer and two of its Florida-based employees for publishing an allegedly defamatory article about her. The article was written and edited entirely in Florida, but it focused on Jones's professional conduct and reputation in California. The defendants argued that they had never set foot in California and that all their work occurred in Florida. Jones countered that the article was aimed at a California audience and caused harm to her reputation where she lived and worked. The question became whether a defendant who commits an intentional act outside the forum can be sued in the forum when the harm is felt there.

Issue

Whether a state may exercise personal jurisdiction over out-of-state defendants who commit intentional acts expressly aimed at the forum state, causing harm that the defendants know will be felt there.

Holding

Yes. When a defendant's intentional conduct is expressly aimed at the forum state and the brunt of the harm is suffered there, personal jurisdiction is proper.

Reasoning

1. **The Effects Test.** The Court held that jurisdiction is proper when the defendant's actions are

intentionally directed at the forum, and the harm is primarily felt there.

2. **Targeting the Forum.** The article focused on a California resident's professional life in California, making the state the focal point of both the story and the harm.
3. **Foreseeability of Harm.** The defendants knew the article would have its greatest impact in California, where Jones lived and worked.
4. **Intentional Conduct Matters.** Unlike accidental or incidental effects, intentional torts aimed at the forum justify jurisdiction.

Final Takeaway

Calder creates the **effects test**: when a defendant intentionally targets the forum and causes harm there, jurisdiction is proper even without physical presence. Think of it as a spotlight — if the defendant shines their conduct directly at the forum, they can be sued where the impact lands.

Keeton v. Hustler Magazine, Inc. (1984)

Narrative Facts

Kathy Keeton, a New York resident, sued Hustler Magazine for libel in New Hampshire. She chose New Hampshire because its statute of limitations was longer than in other states and because Hustler circulated a modest but consistent number of magazines there each month. Keeton herself had no personal or professional ties to New Hampshire. Hustler argued that it should not be sued in a state where the plaintiff had no connection and where the alleged harm did not originate. Keeton countered that Hustler's regular circulation in New Hampshire created sufficient contacts for jurisdiction. The question became whether a defendant's continuous distribution of a publication in a state allows a plaintiff — even a non-resident — to sue there.

Issue

Whether a state may exercise personal jurisdiction over a publisher in a libel action brought by a non-resident plaintiff when the defendant regularly circulates its publication in the forum state.

Holding

Yes. A state may exercise personal jurisdiction over a publisher when the defendant regularly circulates its magazine in the forum, even if the plaintiff has no ties to the state.

Reasoning

1. **Defendant's Contacts Control.** The Court emphasized that jurisdiction depends on the

defendant's contacts with the forum, not the plaintiff's.

2. **Regular Circulation Creates Purposeful Availment.** Hustler's consistent monthly distribution in New Hampshire constituted deliberate engagement with the state's market.

3. **Forum's Interest in Redressing Harm.** New Hampshire had an interest in providing a forum for claims arising from publications circulated within its borders.

4. **Plaintiff's Residency Is Irrelevant.** The Court rejected the idea that a plaintiff must have ties to the forum for jurisdiction to be proper.

Final Takeaway

Keeton reinforces that **jurisdiction turns on the defendant's choices**, not the plaintiff's. When a publisher sends its content into a state month after month, it opens itself to suit there — even by non-residents. Think of it as a rule of distribution: if you spread your product into a forum, you accept the legal consequences that follow.

Shaffer v. Heitner (1977)

Narrative Facts

Heitner, a shareholder of Greyhound Corporation, filed a lawsuit in Delaware alleging that the company's officers and directors had engaged in corporate misconduct. None of the defendants lived in Delaware, and the alleged wrongdoing did not occur there. To establish jurisdiction, Heitner used Delaware's sequestration statute to "attach" the defendants' Greyhound stock — not physical certificates, but the legal fiction that the stock was considered located in Delaware because the corporation was incorporated there. The defendants argued that this was an outdated, artificial way to force them into a Delaware court. The case required the Supreme Court to decide whether the old *Pennoyer*-era rules for quasi in rem jurisdiction survived the modern *International Shoe* minimum-contacts framework.

Issue

Whether a state may exercise quasi in rem jurisdiction based solely on the presence of a defendant's property in the forum when the defendant lacks minimum contacts with the state.

Holding

No. All assertions of state-court jurisdiction — including quasi in rem — must satisfy the *International Shoe* minimum-contacts standard.

Reasoning

1. **Minimum Contacts Apply to All Jurisdiction Types.** The Court held that *International Shoe*

replaced the rigid territorial rules of *Pennoyer*, even for property-based jurisdiction.

2. **Property Presence Is Not Enough.** The mere fact that stock is "located" in Delaware because the corporation is incorporated there does not create meaningful contacts between the defendants and the state.

3. **No Connection to the Forum.** The defendants' alleged misconduct had no link to Delaware, and they had no personal or professional ties to the state.

4. **Fairness and Due Process.** Allowing jurisdiction based on fictional property presence would undermine the fairness principles at the heart of modern due process.

Final Takeaway

Shaffer closes the door on *Pennoyer*'s property-based shortcuts. **All jurisdiction — personal, in rem, and quasi in rem — must meet the minimum-contacts test.** Think of it as the final unification of the doctrine: no matter the form, jurisdiction must be grounded in fairness and real connections, not legal fictions.

Subject Matter Jurisdiction Cases

Subject Matter Jurisdiction defines **what kinds of cases a federal court has the power to hear**. Unlike personal jurisdiction, which focuses on fairness to the defendant, subject matter jurisdiction is about **institutional authority** — the boundaries set by the Constitution and Congress. It cannot be waived, created by consent, or ignored by the court.

The core idea is simple: **Federal courts may only hear the types of cases the Constitution and Congress allow them to hear.**

There are two primary sources of federal subject matter jurisdiction:

> **-Federal Question Jurisdiction** — cases "arising under" federal law, the Constitution, or federal statutes.
>
> **-Diversity Jurisdiction** — cases between citizens of different states where the amount in controversy exceeds the statutory minimum, (under 28U.S.C.§1332(a), the statutory amount in controversy requirement for diversity jurisdiction is "exceeds $75,000.00" this means that claims must be $75,001.00 or more.

Supplemental jurisdiction may allow related state claims to join the case, **but SMJ itself must always be established independently.**

Examples

Example 1: Federal Question (Allowed)

A plaintiff sues under a federal employment statute. Because the claim arises under **federal law**, the federal court has subject matter jurisdiction.

Example 2: Diversity Jurisdiction (Allowed)

Plaintiff is from Wisconsin. Defendant is from Illinois. The amount in controversy is **$100,000**. Because the parties are from different states and the amount exceeds the threshold, the federal court may hear the case.

Example 3: No Federal Question + No Diversity (Not Allowed)

Two parties from Wisconsin dispute a $5,000 contract issue. There is **no federal law** involved and **no diversity**. The case belongs in state court.

Example 4: Federal Claim Disappears (Court May Keep or Dismiss)

A plaintiff brings a federal claim and a related state claim. If the federal claim is dismissed early, the court may choose to dismiss the state claim too — but it also has discretion to keep it if fairness and efficiency support doing so.

Summary

Subject matter jurisdiction asks whether this case is the kind of case federal courts are allowed to hear at all.

Gunn v. Minton (2013)

Narrative Facts

Minton, a Texas lawyer, lost a patent infringement lawsuit and blamed his attorneys for not raising a key argument early enough. He sued them for legal malpractice in Texas state court. His theory was that if the patent issue had been handled differently, he would have won the original case. The defendants argued that because the malpractice claim required analyzing a federal patent question, only federal courts could hear it. Minton insisted that malpractice is a state-law claim and belongs in state court. The dispute forced the Supreme Court to decide whether a state-law claim that contains a federal issue automatically becomes a federal case.

Issue

Whether a state-law legal malpractice claim that requires resolving an underlying federal patent question gives rise to federal subject matter jurisdiction.

Holding

No. A state-law claim does not fall within federal question jurisdiction merely because it involves a federal issue; the federal issue must be substantial to the federal system as a whole.

Reasoning

1. **The Grable Test Applies.** The Court reaffirmed that federal jurisdiction exists over state-law claims only when the federal issue is necessarily raised, actually disputed, substantial, and capable of

resolution in federal court without disrupting the federal-state balance.

2. **Not Substantial to the Federal System.** Although the malpractice claim required analyzing patent law, the outcome would affect only the parties — not the federal patent system.

3. **State Courts Can Apply Federal Law.** The Court emphasized that state courts routinely interpret federal law, and doing so here would not undermine federal interests.

4. **No Federal Forum Needed.** Allowing every malpractice claim involving federal issues into federal court would flood the system and distort jurisdictional boundaries.

Final Takeaway

Gunn clarifies that **not every federal issue creates federal jurisdiction**. The federal question must be important to the federal system itself, not just relevant to the parties. Think of it as a significance test — the issue must matter nationally, not just locally.

Hertz Corp. v. Friend (2010)

Narrative Facts

Two California employees sued Hertz Corporation in California state court, alleging violations of state wage-and-hour laws. Hertz removed the case to federal court, arguing that diversity jurisdiction existed because Hertz was a citizen of New Jersey, not California. The plaintiffs countered that Hertz did substantial business in California — more than in any other state — and therefore should be considered a California citizen. Lower courts struggled with the question: is a corporation's citizenship based on the state where it does the most business, or the state where its true headquarters is located? The Supreme Court took the case to resolve decades of confusion over the meaning of a corporation's "principal place of business."

Issue

How should courts determine a corporation's "principal place of business" for purposes of diversity jurisdiction under 28 U.S.C. § 1332?

Holding

A corporation's principal place of business is its **"nerve center"** — the place where its high-level officers direct, control, and coordinate the company's activities, typically its headquarters.

Reasoning

1. **Need for a Simple, Uniform Test.** The Court rejected multi-factor, business-activity tests as unpredictable and inconsistent across circuits.

2. **The Nerve Center Rule.** The principal place of business is the corporation's actual center of direction and control — usually the headquarters, so long as it is the real decision-making hub.

3. **Avoiding Manipulation.** The Court warned that a corporation cannot manufacture jurisdiction by labeling a nominal office as its headquarters; the nerve center must reflect real operations.

4. **Clarity Promotes Efficiency.** A bright-line rule reduces litigation over jurisdiction and aligns with Congress's intent to keep diversity jurisdiction straightforward.

Final Takeaway

Hertz gives us the modern, streamlined rule: **a corporation lives where its brain lives**. The nerve center test anchors corporate citizenship in a single, identifiable place, bringing clarity to diversity jurisdiction and ending decades of circuit splits.

Arbaugh v. Y&H Corp. (2006)

Narrative Facts

A restaurant employee sued her employer under Title VII, alleging sexual harassment and discrimination. After losing at trial, the employer raised a new argument: the restaurant did not have **15 employees**, meaning it was **not covered** by Title VII. The employer claimed this was a **jurisdictional defect**, meaning the federal court never had the power to hear the case in the first place. The plaintiff argued that the 15-employee requirement was not jurisdictional — it was simply an element of the claim that the employer should have raised earlier. The Supreme Court took the case to clarify when a statutory requirement is truly jurisdictional and when it is merely part of the merits.

Issue

Whether Title VII's 15-employee requirement is a jurisdictional rule that limits federal courts' power, or a non-jurisdictional element of a plaintiff's claim.

Holding

The 15-employee requirement is **not** jurisdictional. It is an element of the plaintiff's claim and must be raised in a timely manner, not after judgment.

Reasoning

1. **Clear Statement Rule.** A requirement is jurisdictional only if Congress clearly states that it limits the court's power.

2. **Title VII Contains No Such Statement.** The statute places the 15-employee requirement in the definitional section, not in the jurisdictional section.

3. **Jurisdiction Cannot Be Created or Destroyed by Waiver.** Because the requirement is not jurisdictional, the employer could not raise it for the first time after losing at trial.

4. **Promoting Fairness and Efficiency.** Treating every statutory requirement as jurisdictional would allow losing parties to ambush courts and litigants after the fact.

Final Takeaway

Arbaugh draws a bright line: **a rule is jurisdictional only if Congress clearly says so**. Everything else is a merits question. This protects litigants from late-stage surprises and keeps jurisdiction focused on true limits of judicial power.

Grable & Sons Metal Products, Inc. v. Darue Engineering & Manufacturing (2005)

Narrative Facts

The IRS seized Grable's property to satisfy a federal tax delinquency and sold it to Darue Engineering. Grable later sued Darue in state court, claiming the IRS had failed to give proper notice of the seizure as required by federal tax law. Darue removed the case to federal court, arguing that the quiet-title action turned entirely on the meaning of a federal statute. Grable insisted that because the claim was created by state law, it belonged in state court. The Supreme Court took the case to clarify when a state-law claim containing a federal issue may be heard in federal court.

Issue

Whether a state-law claim that turns on the interpretation of a federal statute can give rise to federal question jurisdiction under 28 U.S.C. § 1331.

Holding

Yes. A state-law claim may arise under federal law when it necessarily raises a disputed and substantial federal issue that can be resolved in federal court without disrupting the federal-state balance.

Reasoning

1. **Federal Issue Was Necessary and Disputed.** The quiet-title claim depended entirely on whether the IRS complied with a federal notice statute.

2. **Substantial Federal Interest.** The federal government has a strong interest in the uniform interpretation of tax-collection procedures.

3. **Federal Forum Appropriate.** Allowing federal courts to hear such cases would not open the floodgates because these situations are rare and involve important federal questions.

4. **Balancing Federal and State Roles.** The Court emphasized that only a "slim category" of state-law claims qualify — those with genuinely significant federal issues.

Final Takeaway

Grable establishes the modern embedded-federal-issue test: **a state-law claim belongs in federal court only when the federal issue is necessary, actually disputed, substantial to the federal system, and suitable for federal resolution**. Think of it as the doorway to federal court that opens only for issues of true national importance.

Exxon Mobil Corp. v. Allapattah Services, Inc. (2005)

Narrative Facts

Exxon franchisees sued the company in federal court, alleging that Exxon had overcharged them for fuel. One plaintiff met the amount-in-controversy requirement for diversity jurisdiction, but several others did not. The question was whether the federal court could hear the entire case — including the smaller claims — under supplemental jurisdiction. The plaintiffs argued that once one diverse plaintiff satisfied the amount requirement, the rest could "ride along." Exxon countered that each plaintiff must independently meet the $75,000 threshold. The Supreme Court took the case to resolve a long-standing split over the scope of supplemental jurisdiction in diversity cases.

Issue

Whether, in a diversity case, federal courts may exercise supplemental jurisdiction over additional plaintiffs whose claims do not meet the amount-in-controversy requirement when at least one plaintiff does.

Holding

Yes. When at least one plaintiff satisfies the amount-in-controversy requirement and the other elements of diversity jurisdiction are met, federal courts may hear additional plaintiffs' claims under supplemental jurisdiction.

Reasoning

1. **Statutory Text of § 1367.** The Court emphasized that Congress intended supplemental jurisdiction to

be broad, covering all claims that form part of the same case or controversy.

2. **Complete Diversity Still Required.** Supplemental jurisdiction cannot cure a lack of complete diversity, but it can cure a lack of amount in controversy for additional plaintiffs.

3. **Efficiency and Judicial Economy.** Allowing related claims to proceed together avoids duplicative litigation and promotes consistent outcomes.

4. **Congress Overruled Prior Limitations.** The Court noted that § 1367 was enacted to expand supplemental jurisdiction beyond earlier judicial restrictions.

Final Takeaway

Allapattah confirms that **one plaintiff's qualifying claim can anchor the entire case**. As long as complete diversity exists, additional plaintiffs with smaller claims may join under supplemental jurisdiction. Think of it as a jurisdictional umbrella — once one claim opens the door, related claims can follow.

Steel Co. v. Citizens for a Better Environment (1998)

Narrative Facts

Citizens for a Better Environment sued Steel Co. under the Emergency Planning and Community Right-to-Know Act (EPCRA), alleging that the company had failed to file required toxic-chemical reports on time. By the time the lawsuit was filed, Steel Co. had already submitted the missing reports. The plaintiffs sought civil penalties payable to the U.S. Treasury — not to themselves. Steel Co. argued that the plaintiffs lacked **Article III standing** because they had not suffered a concrete injury and would not benefit from the penalties. The lower courts sidestepped the standing question and ruled on the merits instead. The Supreme Court took the case to decide whether federal courts may reach the merits of a case before confirming their own jurisdiction.

Issue

Whether a federal court may decide the merits of a case before determining whether the plaintiff has Article III standing.

Holding

No. A federal court must confirm its jurisdiction — including Article III standing — before addressing the merits of a case.

Reasoning

1. **Jurisdiction First.** The Court held that jurisdiction is a threshold requirement; courts cannot assume jurisdiction to reach the merits.

2. **No Injury, No Standing.** The plaintiffs suffered no concrete injury because the reports were already filed and civil penalties would not redress any harm to them.

3. **No Hypothetical Jurisdiction.** The Court rejected the practice of "hypothetical jurisdiction," where courts assume jurisdiction to resolve a case more easily.

4. **Separation of Powers.** Allowing courts to bypass jurisdictional limits would expand judicial power beyond constitutional boundaries.

Final Takeaway

Steel Co. establishes a strict rule: **federal courts must decide jurisdiction before anything else**. No shortcuts, no hypothetical jurisdiction, no merits-first approach. If standing is missing, the case ends before it begins.

Louisville & Nashville Railroad Co. v. Mottley (1908)

Narrative Facts

The Mottleys were injured in a railroad accident and settled with the railroad by receiving free lifetime passes. Years later, Congress passed a federal statute prohibiting railroads from issuing free passes. When the railroad refused to honor the Mottleys' passes, they sued in federal court seeking specific performance of the original settlement. Their complaint anticipated that the railroad would defend itself by citing the federal statute — and the Mottleys argued that this anticipated federal defense created federal question jurisdiction. The Supreme Court took the case to decide whether a federal issue raised only in anticipation of a defense is enough to bring a case into federal court.

Issue

Whether a federal court has federal question jurisdiction when the federal issue appears only as an anticipated defense, rather than on the face of the plaintiff's well-pleaded complaint.

Holding

No. A federal question must appear on the face of the plaintiff's well-pleaded complaint; a federal defense does not create federal jurisdiction.

Reasoning

1. **The Well-Pleaded Complaint Rule.** Jurisdiction depends solely on what the plaintiff must allege to

state their claim — not on defenses the defendant might raise.

2. **Anticipated Defenses Are Irrelevant.** Even if the defendant's defense is based on federal law, that does not convert the case into a federal question case.

3. **Protecting the Limits of Federal Power.** Allowing federal defenses to create jurisdiction would dramatically expand federal court authority beyond what Congress intended.

4. **Plaintiff Controls the Claim.** The plaintiff chooses the theory of the case; if the claim arises under state law, the case belongs in state court.

Final Takeaway

Mottley is the cornerstone of federal question doctrine: **the federal issue must be part of the plaintiff's own claim**, not a defense. This rule keeps federal courts from being flooded with cases that only tangentially involve federal law.

Osborn v. Bank of the United States (1824)

Narrative Facts

The Bank of the United States sued Osborn, the Ohio state auditor, after he attempted to collect a state tax that the Bank argued was unconstitutional. The case arose during a period of intense political conflict over the Bank's legitimacy. Congress had authorized the Bank to "sue and be sued" in federal court, but Ohio argued that this language did not automatically create federal jurisdiction. The dispute forced the Supreme Court to confront a foundational question: **How broad is federal question jurisdiction under Article III, and how much federal content is needed to bring a case into federal court?**

Issue

Whether Congress may grant federal jurisdiction over any case involving a federally chartered entity by including a "sue and be sued" clause, even when the underlying dispute does not necessarily arise under federal law.

Holding

Yes. Congress may grant federal jurisdiction over cases involving federally chartered entities, and Article III allows federal courts to hear any case with a federal "ingredient," even if the federal issue is not the primary dispute.

Reasoning

1. **The Federal-Ingredient Theory.** Chief Justice Marshall held that a case arises under federal law whenever federal law forms an essential part of the

controversy, even if the claim itself is grounded in state law.

2. **Congress's Power to Create Jurisdiction.** Congress may authorize federal courts to hear cases involving federal institutions because such cases inherently implicate federal interests.
3. **Breadth of Article III.** Article III's "arising under" language is broader than the statutory grant of federal question jurisdiction; it encompasses any case with a federal component.
4. **National Interests at Stake.** Disputes involving federal entities often require uniform federal interpretation, justifying federal jurisdiction.

Final Takeaway

Osborn establishes the **federal-ingredient doctrine**: a case may arise under federal law even when the federal issue is not the main claim. Although modern statutory jurisdiction is narrower, Osborn remains the constitutional foundation for understanding the outer limits of federal judicial power.

SUPPLEMENTAL SUBJECT MATTER JURISDICTION CASES

These cases refine the boundaries of supplemental jurisdiction and complete diversity, showing how federal and state claims can travel together in a single lawsuit — and where the limits are. They clarify when a federal court may hear related state claims, when adding parties destroys diversity, and how § 1367 shapes the structure of multi-claim litigation.

Summary: These cases explain when federal courts may hear related state claims and when jurisdictional limits prevent it.

United Mine Workers v. Gibbs (1966)

Narrative Facts

Gibbs was hired to manage a coal-loading operation in Tennessee. When the United Mine Workers union became involved in a labor dispute, violence and threats erupted, and Gibbs lost both his job and a related trucking contract. He sued the union in federal court, bringing **both** a federal claim under labor law and **state-law tort claims** for interference with contract and business relations. The federal claim ultimately failed, leaving only the state claims. The question became whether the federal court could still hear the state-law claims once the federal claim dropped out.

Issue

Whether federal courts may hear state-law claims that are related to a federal claim, even if the federal claim is later dismissed.

Holding

Yes. Federal courts may exercise pendent (now supplemental) jurisdiction over state-law claims that arise from a **common nucleus of operative fact** with the federal claim, but they have discretion to decline jurisdiction if the federal claim is dismissed early.

Reasoning

1. **Common Nucleus of Operative Fact.** State and federal claims belong together when they arise from

the same set of facts such that a plaintiff would ordinarily try them in one proceeding.

2. **Judicial Economy and Fairness.** Hearing related claims together avoids duplication, inconsistent judgments, and unnecessary expense.

3. **Discretion to Decline.** If the federal claim is dismissed early, the court may — but is not required to — dismiss the state claims as well.

4. **Federalism Concerns.** State courts should decide state-law issues when the federal interest is no longer present.

Final Takeaway

Gibbs establishes the modern test for supplemental jurisdiction: **if the claims share a common nucleus of operative fact, they form one constitutional case**. But federal courts retain discretion — supplemental jurisdiction is permitted, not mandatory.

Owen Equipment & Erection Co. v. Kroger (1978)

Narrative Facts

Kroger, an Iowa resident, sued the Omaha Public Power District (OPPD) in federal court based on diversity jurisdiction. During the litigation, Kroger added a new defendant: Owen Equipment. At first, everyone believed Owen was a Nebraska citizen, which would preserve diversity. Later, it turned out that Owen was actually incorporated in **Iowa** — the same state as Kroger. This destroyed complete diversity. Kroger argued that the court could still hear the claim under **pendent party jurisdiction** (what we now call supplemental jurisdiction). Owen countered that allowing this would undermine the complete-diversity rule. The Supreme Court took the case to decide whether supplemental jurisdiction can be used to add a non-diverse defendant in a diversity case.

Issue

Whether a federal court sitting in diversity may exercise supplemental jurisdiction over a claim by a plaintiff against a non-diverse third-party defendant.

Holding

No. Supplemental jurisdiction cannot be used to circumvent the requirement of **complete diversity**. A plaintiff may not use supplemental jurisdiction to bring a claim against a non-diverse party.

Reasoning

1. **Complete Diversity Is Mandatory.** The Court reaffirmed that diversity jurisdiction requires every plaintiff to be diverse from every defendant.
2. **Plaintiff Cannot Expand Jurisdiction.** A plaintiff who chooses federal court cannot later add a non-diverse defendant and rely on supplemental jurisdiction to keep the case there.
3. **Preventing Strategic Manipulation.** Allowing plaintiffs to add non-diverse defendants would undermine the purpose of diversity jurisdiction and invite gamesmanship.
4. **Different from Impleader Situations.** The Court distinguished cases where defendants bring in third parties — those situations may allow supplemental jurisdiction because the plaintiff did not choose the additional party.

Final Takeaway

Owen sets a firm boundary: **supplemental jurisdiction cannot cure a lack of complete diversity when the plaintiff is the one adding the non-diverse party**. Think of it as a one-way door — defendants may bring in related parties, but plaintiffs cannot use supplemental jurisdiction to expand the case beyond the limits of diversity.

Strawbridge v. Curtiss (1806)

Narrative Facts

In an early dispute involving land and debt, multiple plaintiffs sued multiple defendants in federal court under diversity jurisdiction. Some plaintiffs were citizens of the same state as some defendants. The Judiciary Act of 1789 allowed federal courts to hear cases "between citizens of different states," but the statute did not specify whether **every** plaintiff had to be diverse from **every** defendant. The Supreme Court was asked to interpret the statute and determine how strictly diversity should be applied.

Issue

Whether diversity jurisdiction requires **complete diversity** — meaning every plaintiff must be diverse from every defendant — or whether "minimal diversity" is enough.

Holding

Complete diversity is required. No plaintiff may share state citizenship with any defendant.

Reasoning

1. **Interpretation of the Judiciary Act.** The Court read the statute as requiring full separation of citizenship between all plaintiffs and all defendants.
2. **Narrow Construction of Federal Jurisdiction.** Because federal courts are courts of limited jurisdiction, the statute must be interpreted conservatively.

3. **Avoiding Overexpansion.** Allowing minimal diversity would dramatically increase the number of cases in federal court, contrary to Congress's intent.

4. **Bright-Line Rule.** The Court established a clear, administrable rule that has guided diversity jurisdiction ever since.

Final Takeaway

Strawbridge gives us the foundational rule: **complete diversity is mandatory** unless Congress explicitly provides otherwise. This case anchors the entire structure of diversity jurisdiction and remains controlling law today.

VENUE & TRANSFER THROUGH CASES

Venue determines **which federal court is the proper location for a lawsuit**. While subject matter jurisdiction asks *whether* a federal court may hear a case, and personal jurisdiction asks *whether* the court may exercise power over the defendant, **venue asks where within the federal system the case should be filed**.

The core idea is simple: **Venue ensures the case is heard in a fair, convenient, and logically connected place.**

Under the federal venue statute (28 U.S.C. § 1391), a case may be filed in:

- A district where **any defendant resides**, if all defendants live in the same state
- A district where a **substantial part of the events** giving rise to the claim occurred
- If no district fits, any district where the defendant is subject to personal jurisdiction

Sometimes a case is filed in a proper venue but would be **more convenient** elsewhere. That's where **transfer** comes in.

Under 28 U.S.C. § 1404(a), a federal court may transfer a case to another federal district for the convenience of parties and witnesses, and in the interest of justice. Under 28 U.S.C. § 1406(a), if venue is improper, the court may dismiss or transfer the case to a proper venue.

Examples

Example 1: Proper Venue (Events Occurred There)

A car accident happens in the Northern District of Illinois. Even if the defendant lives in Indiana, venue is proper in the Northern District of Illinois because **the events occurred there**.

Example 2: Proper Venue (Defendant's Residence)

Two defendants both live in Wisconsin. The plaintiff sues in the Eastern District of Wisconsin. Venue is proper because **all defendants reside in the same state**, and the district is within that state.

Example 3: Improper Venue → Transfer or Dismissal

A plaintiff files in the District of Arizona, but the defendant lives in Florida and the events happened in Georgia. Arizona has **no connection** to the case. The court may **transfer** the case to Georgia or Florida or dismiss it.

Example 4: Convenience Transfer (1404(a))

A case is properly filed in New York, but most witnesses, documents, and events are in Texas. The court may transfer the case to Texas because it is **more convenient** and serves the **interests of justice**.

Summary

Venue chooses the right federal district for the case, and transfer moves the case to a more appropriate or convenient district when fairness or efficiency requires it.

Atlantic Marine Construction Co. v. U.S. District Court (2013)

Narrative Facts

Atlantic Marine, a Virginia company, hired a Texas subcontractor to work on a construction project. Their contract included a **forum-selection clause** requiring all disputes to be litigated in **Virginia**. When a dispute arose, the subcontractor sued in **Texas federal court** instead. Atlantic Marine moved to transfer the case to Virginia under 28 U.S.C. § 1404(a). The district court refused, reasoning that the plaintiff's choice of forum deserved deference. The Fifth Circuit agreed. The Supreme Court took the case to clarify how § 1404(a) operates when the parties have agreed to a forum-selection clause.

Issue

How should courts apply § 1404(a) when the parties have a valid forum-selection clause pointing to a different federal district?

Holding

A valid forum-selection clause should be **given controlling weight** in all but the most exceptional cases. The case should ordinarily be transferred to the contractually chosen forum.

Reasoning

1. **Plaintiff's Choice Loses Its Privilege.** When the parties agreed to a forum in advance, the plaintiff's choice of a different forum deserves no weight.

2. **Private-Interest Factors Are Off the Table.** The parties already bargained for convenience; only public-interest factors remain, and they rarely defeat transfer.

3. **Choice-of-Law Rules Do Not Travel.** After transfer, the transferee court applies its own choice-of-law rules, preventing plaintiffs from forum-shopping for favorable law.

4. **Enforcing Bargains Promotes Certainty.** Forum-selection clauses create predictability and reduce litigation over venue.

Final Takeaway

Atlantic Marine transforms transfer analysis: **a forum-selection clause flips the usual § 1404(a) framework.** The chosen forum controls unless extraordinary circumstances exist.

Piper Aircraft Co. v. Reyno (1981)

Narrative Facts

A plane manufactured by Piper Aircraft (U.S.) and fitted with a Hartzell propeller (U.S.) crashed in Scotland, killing several Scottish citizens. Their families sued Piper and Hartzell in **California state court**, even though the accident, victims, witnesses, and evidence were all in Scotland. The defendants removed the case to federal court and sought dismissal under **forum non conveniens**, arguing that Scotland was the far more appropriate forum. The district court agreed. The Ninth Circuit reversed, reasoning that Scottish law was less favorable to plaintiffs, and therefore dismissal would be unfair. The Supreme Court took the case to clarify how courts should evaluate forum non conveniens motions.

Issue

Whether a court may dismiss a case under forum non conveniens when the alternative forum's law is less favorable to the plaintiff.

Holding

Yes. A court may dismiss for forum non conveniens even if the alternative forum's law is less favorable, so long as the alternative forum is adequate and the private and public interest factors strongly favor dismissal.

Reasoning

1. **Adequate Alternative Forum.** Scotland was an adequate forum because the defendants were amenable to process there and Scottish courts could hear the claims.

2. **Private-Interest Factors.** Evidence, witnesses, accident site, and relevant documents were all in Scotland — making trial in the U.S. inefficient and burdensome.

3. **Public-Interest Factors.** Scotland had a far stronger interest in regulating its own aviation accidents; U.S. courts should not be overloaded with foreign disputes.

4. **No Right to the Most Favorable Law.** The Court rejected the idea that plaintiffs can avoid dismissal simply because another forum's law is less generous.

Final Takeaway

Piper establishes the modern rule: **forum non conveniens focuses on convenience and fairness, not on which forum offers better law**. If the alternative forum is adequate and the balance of interests strongly favors it, dismissal is appropriate.

Hoffman v. Blaski (1960)

Narrative Facts

Blaski sued several defendants in federal court in Texas. The defendants wanted the case transferred to Illinois under 28 U.S.C. § 1404(a), arguing that Illinois would be a more convenient forum. The plaintiffs objected, pointing out that the defendants could not have originally been sued in Illinois because venue and personal jurisdiction were lacking there at the time the lawsuit was filed. The lower courts approved the transfer anyway, reasoning that the defendants were now willing to waive objections to venue and jurisdiction. The Supreme Court took the case to decide whether a case may be transferred to a district where it **could not originally have been brought**, simply because the defendant consents.

Issue

Whether a federal court may transfer a case under § 1404(a) to a district where the plaintiff could not originally have filed the lawsuit, based solely on the defendant's consent.

Holding

No. A case may be transferred only to a district where the plaintiff **could have originally filed** the action. Defendant consent cannot create proper venue or jurisdiction.

Reasoning

1. **Statutory Text Controls.** Section 1404(a) allows transfer only to a district "where the action **might have been brought**." This refers to the plaintiff's rights at the time of filing, not the defendant's later preferences.

2. **Defendant Consent Is Irrelevant.** Venue and jurisdiction must exist independently; they cannot be manufactured by waiver or agreement.
3. **Protecting Plaintiff's Filing Choices.** Allowing defendants to force transfer to an otherwise improper forum would undermine the plaintiff's statutory rights.
4. **Preventing Strategic Manipulation.** Without this rule, defendants could steer cases to forums that were originally unavailable, distorting the venue system.

Final Takeaway

Hoffman establishes a bright-line rule: **a case can be transferred only to a district where it could have been filed originally**. Convenience cannot override statutory venue requirements, and defendant consent cannot cure an improper transferee forum.

ERIE DOCTRINE THROUGH CASES

The Erie Doctrine governs **what law federal courts apply** when sitting in diversity. It is the backbone of federalism in civil litigation, balancing state authority, federal procedure, and the constitutional limits of judicial power.

A Simple, Clear Explanation of Erie Doctrine

When a case is in federal court **because the parties are from different states** (diversity jurisdiction), the federal court must apply:

- **State substantive law**
- **Federal procedural law**

This rule comes from *Erie Railroad Co. v. Tompkins*, 304 U.S. 64 (1938).

Think of it this way:

State law provides the recipe. Federal law provides the kitchen rules.

- **State substantive law = the ingredients**. These are the actual rights, duties, and remedies – what goes into the case. For example, whether negligence requires duty, breach, causation, and damages, or how damages are calculated.
- **Federal procedural law = the cooking instructions.** These are the steps for how the case is handled in court – deadlines, motions, jury selection,

evidence rules. They don't change what the "meal" is, but they dictate how it is prepared and served.

Federal courts cannot invent their own substantive law. They must respect the state's choices about rights, duties, and remedies.

<u>The Outcome-Determinative Test</u> - (Guaranty Trust Co. v. York)

The key question: **Would applying the state rule instead of the federal rule change the outcome of the case?**

If **yes,** the rule is outcome-determinative — and the federal court should apply the **state** rule to avoid:

- **Forum shopping** (choosing federal court for a better rule)
- **Unfairness** (different results in state vs. federal court)

Example (Outcome-Determinative):

- State statute of limitations: **3 years**
- Federal rule: **4 years**
- Plaintiff files at **3.5 years**

Under state law → **case dismissed** Under federal rule → **case survives**

Because the result changes, the state rule must apply.

Example (Not Outcome-Determinative):

- State requires **blue ink** on the cover sheet

- Federal requires **black ink**

Either way → **the case proceeds**

The rule does not affect the outcome, so the **federal procedural rule** applies.

Putting It All Together

- **If the rule affects the result → apply state law.**
- **If the rule does not affect the result → apply federal procedural law.**

This preserves fairness, prevents strategic manipulation, and keeps federal courts from undermining state policy choices.

Gasperini v. Center for Humanities (1996)

Narrative Facts

Gasperini, a journalist, sued the Center for Humanities after valuable photographic slides were lost. A federal jury in New York awarded him substantial damages. New York state law, however, required courts to reduce verdicts that "deviate materially" from reasonable compensation — a stricter standard than the traditional federal "shocks the conscience" test. The question was whether a federal court sitting in diversity must apply New York's damages-review standard, or whether federal procedural rules controlled. The case forced the Supreme Court to confront the tension between **state substantive policy** and **federal procedural structure**.

Issue

Whether a federal court sitting in diversity must apply a state law standard for reviewing excessive jury verdicts.

Holding

Yes. The state's "deviates materially" standard is substantive and must be applied by federal courts, but the federal appellate standard of review remains intact.

Reasoning

1. **State Standard Is Substantive.** New York's rule reflects a substantive policy choice about the proper size of damages awards.

2. **Federal Structure Must Be Preserved.** While the district court must apply the state standard, the federal appellate court must still use the federal "abuse of discretion" review.

3. **Balancing Federalism and Procedure.** The Court sought to harmonize Erie's twin aims — discouraging forum shopping and avoiding inequitable administration of the laws — without undermining federal judicial structure.

4. **No Displacement of Federal Rules.** Because no Federal Rule of Civil Procedure directly conflicted with the state standard, the state rule applied.

Final Takeaway

Gasperini shows Erie's modern nuance: **state substantive policies apply, but federal courts retain their procedural architecture**. It is a doctrine of balance, not absolutism.

Hanna v. Plumer (1965)

Narrative Facts

A woman died in a car accident, and her executor sued the defendant in federal court based on diversity jurisdiction. Service of process became the central issue. The plaintiff served the defendant's **wife** at their home, following **Federal Rule of Civil Procedure 4**, which allowed substituted service. But Massachusetts state law required **personal, in-hand service** on the defendant himself. The defendant argued that because this was a diversity case, the federal court had to follow state service rules under the Erie Doctrine. The Supreme Court took the case to decide what happens when a **Federal Rule of Civil Procedure directly conflicts with state law**.

Issue

When a Federal Rule of Civil Procedure conflicts with a state law in a diversity case, which one controls?

Holding

The Federal Rule controls, so long as it is valid under the Rules Enabling Act and does not violate the Constitution.

Reasoning

1. **Direct Conflict Means Federal Rule Wins.** When a Federal Rule squarely addresses the issue, the Erie analysis shifts — the Federal Rule governs if it is valid.

2. **Rules Enabling Act Test.** A Federal Rule is valid if it regulates **procedure**, not substantive rights. Rule 4 clearly regulates procedure.

3. **Erie's Twin Aims Are Secondary Here.** The twin aims — avoiding forum shopping and inequitable administration — apply only when no Federal Rule is on point.

4. **Uniform Federal Procedure.** The Court emphasized the importance of consistent federal procedural rules across all federal courts.

Final Takeaway

Hanna gives us the modern framework: **If a Federal Rule directly conflicts with state law, the Federal Rule governs — as long as it is procedural and valid.** This is the backbone of modern Erie analysis.

Byrd v. Blue Ridge Rural Electric Cooperative (1958)

Narrative Facts

Byrd, a construction worker, was injured while working on a power line in South Carolina. He sued the electric cooperative in federal court under diversity jurisdiction. The defendant argued that under **South Carolina law**, the question of whether Byrd was a "statutory employee" (and therefore limited to workers' compensation) had to be decided by a **judge**, not a jury. Federal practice, however, strongly favored jury determination of such factual issues. The case forced the Supreme Court to confront a new problem: **What happens when state law and federal judicial structure point in different directions?**

Issue

When state law assigns a factual determination to a judge, but federal practice assigns it to a jury, which rule governs in a federal diversity case?

Holding

Federal courts may apply federal practice — even if it conflicts with state law — when strong federal interests in the federal judicial system outweigh the state's interest.

Reasoning

1. **State Rule Not Outcome-Determinative Enough.** Applying the state rule would not significantly affect the outcome in a way that implicates Erie's twin aims.

2. **Strong Federal Interest in Jury Trials.** The federal system has a constitutionally rooted commitment to jury fact-finding, especially in civil cases.

3. **Balancing Test Introduced.** The Court weighed the state's interest in uniform workers' compensation administration against the federal interest in preserving the federal court's allocation of functions.

4. **Federal Structure Prevails.** Because the federal interest was substantial, the federal practice controlled.

Final Takeaway

Byrd adds a new dimension to Erie: **even when state law is substantive, federal courts may follow federal practice if strong federal interests are at stake**. It introduces a balancing test that tempers the rigidity of earlier Erie cases.

Guaranty Trust Co. v. York (1945)

Narrative Facts

York sued Guaranty Trust in federal court on a state-law claim involving alleged fiduciary breaches. The problem? The claim was **time-barred** under the state statute of limitations. York argued that federal courts sitting in equity were not bound by state limitation periods and could apply their own equitable doctrines. The defendant countered that allowing federal courts to ignore state statutes of limitations would produce radically different outcomes depending on whether a case was filed in state or federal court. The Supreme Court took the case to clarify how Erie applies when state law would extinguish the claim entirely.

Issue

Must a federal court sitting in diversity apply a state statute of limitations, even when the case is brought in equity?

Holding

Yes. A federal court must apply the state statute of limitations because failing to do so would substantially affect the outcome of the case.

Reasoning

1. **Outcome-Determinative Test Introduced.** The Court held that if ignoring a state rule would significantly change the outcome of the case, the federal court must apply the state rule.

2. **Equity vs. Law Distinction Rejected.** Erie applies equally to legal and equitable claims; federal courts cannot revive claims that state law has extinguished.

3. **Preventing Forum Shopping.** If plaintiffs could avoid state statutes of limitations by filing in federal court, it would encourage strategic forum selection.
4. **Uniformity and Fairness.** The same claim should produce the same result whether filed in state or federal court.

Final Takeaway

Guaranty Trust crystallizes the **outcome-determinative test: If applying federal practice instead of state law would change the result, the state rule must apply.** This case pushes Erie toward a strong preference for state law in diversity cases.

Erie Railroad Co. v. Tompkins (1938)

Narrative Facts

On a dark Pennsylvania night, Tompkins was walking along a footpath beside the Erie Railroad tracks when a passing train struck him with a protruding object, severing his arm. He sued the railroad in **federal court in New York**, invoking diversity jurisdiction. Under Pennsylvania state law, Tompkins was considered a **trespasser**, and the railroad owed him only a minimal duty of care — meaning he would likely lose. But under the federal "general common law" created by *Swift v. Tyson*, Tompkins could argue for a more generous negligence standard. The federal court applied federal general common law and awarded him damages. The Supreme Court took the case to decide whether federal courts could continue creating their own general common law in diversity cases.

Issue

May federal courts apply a federal "general common law" in diversity cases, or must they apply state substantive law?

Holding

Federal courts may **not** create or apply general federal common law in diversity cases. They must apply **state substantive law**, including state judicial decisions.

Reasoning

1. **Swift Was Wrongly Decided.** The Court held that *Swift v. Tyson* had led to grave injustices and encouraged forum shopping.

2. **No Federal General Common Law.** The Constitution does not authorize federal courts to create general common law; only Congress can make federal law.

3. **State Judicial Decisions Are State Law.** State common law is as binding as state statutes for Erie purposes.

4. **Federalism and Equality.** Litigants should not obtain different outcomes simply by choosing federal court over state court.

Final Takeaway

Erie is a constitutional revolution: **Federal courts must apply state substantive law in diversity cases.** It ends the era of federal general common law and anchors modern federalism.

Swift v. Tyson (1842)

Narrative Facts

A dispute over a bill of exchange brought Swift, a New York citizen, into federal court against Tyson, a Maine citizen. The case turned on whether Tyson had given value for the bill — a question governed by **commercial law**. Instead of applying New York state court decisions, Justice Story announced that federal courts sitting in diversity were free to apply a **federal general common law** in areas like commercial transactions. This meant that federal courts could disregard state judicial decisions and instead craft their own rules. For nearly a century, this doctrine shaped federal diversity practice — and created the very problems that *Erie* later dismantled.

Issue

Whether federal courts sitting in diversity must apply state judicial decisions as "state law," or whether they may develop a separate body of federal general common law.

Holding

Federal courts may apply a federal general common law in diversity cases and are not bound by state court decisions on general commercial matters.

Reasoning

1. **Distinction Between Local and General Law.** Justice Story held that state court decisions on "general" matters (like commercial law) were not binding on federal courts.

2. **Uniformity in Commercial Law.** The Court believed national uniformity in commercial rules was

desirable and would promote economic development.

3. **Federal Courts as Independent Lawmakers.** The decision assumed federal courts had inherent authority to articulate general common law principles.

4. **State Judicial Decisions Not Treated as Law.** Story treated state court decisions as evidence of law, not law itself — a view later rejected in *Erie.*

Final Takeaway

Swift created the era of **federal general common law**, allowing federal courts to disregard state judicial decisions in many areas. It produced massive forum shopping and inequitable outcomes — the very evils that *Erie* later corrected. Understanding Swift is essential because **Erie is its direct repudiation**.

PLEADING THROUGH CASES

The pleading doctrine answers a deceptively simple question:

What must a plaintiff allege in a complaint for the case to survive a motion to dismiss under Rule 12(b)(6)?

"Failure to state a claim upon which relief can be granted." Federal Rule of Civil Procedure 12(b)(6) – A defendant may move to dismiss a complaint for failure to state a claim upon which relief can be granted. The court assumes the facts are true, but ask: "Even so, does the law allow relief?"

Example:

Plaintiff's claim: "The company fired me unfairly."

Missing: No facts showing discrimination, breach of contract or retaliation.

Result: Dismissed under Fed.R.Civ.P. 12(b)(6) because unfairness alone isn't a legal violation.

To survive a 12(b)(6) motion, the complaint must:

-identify a **legal theory** (e.g., negligence, breach of contract)

-include facts that support each element of the theory.

-avoid vague or conclusory statements (e.g., "The defendant was mean" isn't enough).

Ashcroft v. Iqbal (2009)

Narrative Facts

After the September 11 attacks, Javaid Iqbal, a Pakistani Muslim, was detained in a federal facility under harsh conditions. He sued high-ranking federal officials — including Attorney General Ashcroft and FBI Director Mueller — alleging unconstitutional discrimination. The complaint claimed the officials "knew of, condoned, and willfully and maliciously agreed to" the discriminatory treatment. The government moved to dismiss, arguing that these were **bare conclusions**, not factual allegations. The Supreme Court took the case to clarify how courts should evaluate complaints under Rule 8 after *Twombly*.

Issue

What must a complaint contain to state a plausible claim for relief under Rule 8?

Holding

A complaint must contain **non-conclusory factual allegations** that make the claim **plausible**, not merely possible. Legal conclusions are not entitled to the assumption of truth.

Reasoning

1. **Two-Step Approach.**

    -Identify and disregard conclusory allegations.

    -Evaluate whether the remaining factual allegations plausibly suggest liability.

2. **Plausibility Standard.** The facts must allow the court to draw a reasonable inference of liability — not just speculate.
3. **High-Level Officials Require Specific Facts.** Claims against senior officials cannot rest on generalized assertions of knowledge or intent.
4. **Rule 8 Requires More Than Labels.** The complaint must show, not just allege, entitlement to relief.

Final Takeaway

Iqbal cements the modern rule: **only factual allegations count**, and they must make liability **plausible**, not merely conceivable. This is the definitive articulation of the plausibility standard.

Bell Atlantic Corp. v. Twombly (2007)

Narrative Facts

Consumers brought a class action against major telecommunications companies, alleging that the companies had engaged in an illegal conspiracy to restrain trade. The complaint claimed the companies "agreed not to compete" and engaged in "parallel conduct." But it offered **no specific facts** showing an actual agreement — only behavior that could just as easily be explained by lawful business decisions. The defendants moved to dismiss, arguing that the complaint lacked factual allegations supporting the existence of a conspiracy. The Supreme Court took the case to decide what Rule 8 requires for a complaint to survive a motion to dismiss.

Issue

Does a complaint that alleges only parallel conduct, without factual allegations suggesting an actual agreement, state a claim under Rule 8?

Holding

No. A complaint must contain **enough factual matter** to state a claim that is **plausible**, not merely conceivable. Allegations of parallel conduct, without more, do not meet this standard.

Reasoning

1. **Plausibility Standard Introduced.** The Court held that Rule 8 requires enough facts to "nudge" a claim from conceivable to plausible.

2. **Bare Assertions Are Insufficient.** Labels, conclusions, and formulaic recitations of elements do not satisfy Rule 8.

3. **Parallel Conduct ≠ Conspiracy.** Parallel business behavior is consistent with lawful competition; without additional facts, it does not plausibly suggest an illegal agreement.

4. **Discovery Cannot Be a Fishing Expedition.** The Court emphasized that plaintiffs cannot use vague allegations to force defendants into expensive discovery.

Final Takeaway

Twombly rewrites the pleading landscape: **A complaint must contain factual allegations that make liability plausible — not speculative, not possible, but plausible.** This case sets the stage for *Iqbal*, which universalizes the plausibility standard across all civil cases.

Conley v. Gibson (1957)

Narrative Facts

African-American railroad workers in Texas alleged that their union failed to represent them fairly and allowed white workers to take their jobs. They sued in federal court, claiming racial discrimination and breach of the union's duty of fair representation. The union moved to dismiss, arguing that the complaint lacked detailed facts and failed to specify exactly how the discrimination occurred. The Supreme Court took the case to decide how much detail Rule 8 requires in a complaint.

Issue

Does Rule 8 require plaintiffs to plead detailed facts, or is a short and plain statement of the claim sufficient?

Holding

A short and plain statement is enough. A complaint should not be dismissed unless it appears **beyond doubt** that the plaintiff can prove **no set of facts** in support of the claim.

Reasoning

1. **Notice Pleading.** Rule 8 requires only enough information to give the defendant fair notice of the claim and the grounds upon which it rests.
2. **No Technical Forms Required.** The Federal Rules were designed to simplify pleading and avoid the rigid formalism of common-law and code pleading.

3. **Discovery Fills the Gaps.** The Court emphasized that details can be developed through discovery; the complaint need not contain them.

4. **Extremely Lenient Standard.** The "no set of facts" language created a highly permissive threshold for surviving a motion to dismiss.

Final Takeaway

Conley represents the **high-water mark of notice pleading**: **A complaint survived unless there was no imaginable set of facts that could support the claim.** This forgiving standard governed for 50 years — until *Twombly* and *Iqbal* replaced it with the modern plausibility requirement.

SUMMARY JUDGMENT THROUGH CASES

Summary judgment under Rule 56 asks a single, powerful question:

Is there any genuine dispute of material fact requiring a jury, or can the court decide the case as a matter of law?

"Summary judgment shall be granted if there is no genuine dispute as to any material fact and the movant is entitled to judgment as a matter of law." — Fed. R. Civ. P. 56(a)

This means that if the facts are clear and undisputed, and the law favors one side, the judge can decide the case without a trial.

Example:

There is a bill dispute:

-party A shows a signed receipt.

-party B admits they got the receipt.

There is no real dispute.

Example:

-Plaintiff: "You breached our contract."

-Defendant: "Here's the signed cancellation agreement."

Court: No dispute. Defendant wins on summary judgment.

How it works:

-Who can file: Either party – plaintiff or defendant

-When: Usually after discovery (when both sides have exchanged evidence).

-What the judge looks for:

-Are the facts undisputed?

-Does the law clearly favor one side?

-If yes, the judge grants summary judgment; if no, the case goes to trial.

Celotex Corp. v. Catrett (1986)

Narrative Facts

Catrett sued Celotex, alleging her husband died from exposure to Celotex's asbestos products. Celotex moved for summary judgment, arguing that Catrett had **no evidence** showing exposure to its products. Celotex did **not** produce affirmative evidence disproving exposure; instead, it argued that the plaintiff had failed to produce evidence supporting an essential element of her claim. The lower courts disagreed, insisting Celotex had to produce evidence negating exposure. The Supreme Court took the case to clarify what a moving party must show to win summary judgment.

Issue

May a party moving for summary judgment prevail by showing that the non-moving party lacks evidence on an essential element, even without producing its own evidence?

Holding

Yes. A party may win summary judgment by showing that the non-moving party has **no evidence** to support an essential element of the claim.

Reasoning

1. **Burden of Production, Not Persuasion.** The moving party need only point out the absence of evidence; it does not need to disprove the claim.

2. **Shift to the Non-Movant.** Once the movant identifies the evidentiary gap, the burden shifts to the non-movant to produce admissible evidence.

3. **Rule 56 Is Not a Trial.** Summary judgment is designed to weed out cases lacking evidentiary support before trial.
4. **Efficiency and Fairness.** Requiring defendants to disprove claims would undermine the purpose of summary judgment.

Final Takeaway

Celotex establishes that **a defendant can win summary judgment by showing the plaintiff has no evidence**, without producing contrary evidence. This is the cornerstone of modern summary judgment practice.

Anderson v. Liberty Lobby, Inc. (1986)

Narrative Facts

Liberty Lobby, a political advocacy organization, sued a journalist for libel. Because libel involving public figures requires proof of **actual malice** by **clear and convincing evidence**, the defendant moved for summary judgment, arguing that the plaintiff had not produced evidence meeting that heightened standard. The lower courts disagreed about how to evaluate the evidence at the summary judgment stage. The Supreme Court took the case to clarify what counts as a **"genuine dispute of material fact"** under Rule 56 — especially when the underlying claim requires a heightened burden of proof at trial.

Issue

When deciding a motion for summary judgment, must a court consider the **substantive evidentiary burden** (e.g., clear and convincing evidence) that the plaintiff must meet at trial?

Holding

Yes. A court must consider the **quality and quantity of evidence** required by the substantive law. A dispute is "genuine" only if a reasonable jury could find for the non-movant under the applicable burden of proof.

Reasoning

1. **Materiality Depends on Substantive Law.** A fact is material only if it affects the outcome under the governing legal standard.

2. **Genuineness Requires More Than a Scintilla.** The non-movant must produce evidence sufficient for a reasonable jury to find in their favor.

3. **Burden of Proof Matters.** When the substantive law requires clear and convincing evidence, the court must evaluate whether the evidence meets that threshold.

4. **No Jury Needed for Speculation.** If the evidence is so weak that no reasonable jury could find for the non-movant, summary judgment is appropriate.

Final Takeaway

Anderson defines **what counts as a genuine dispute**: **A dispute is genuine only if a reasonable jury can find for the non-movant under the correct burden of proof.** This case ties summary judgment directly to the substantive evidentiary standard.

Matsushita Electric Industrial Co. v. Zenith Radio Corp. (1986)

Narrative Facts

American electronics companies, including Zenith, sued several Japanese manufacturers, alleging a massive, decades-long conspiracy to drive U.S. companies out of the market through predatory pricing. The defendants moved for summary judgment, arguing that the plaintiffs' theory made no economic sense and that the plaintiffs had not produced evidence supporting a plausible conspiracy. The plaintiffs pointed to ambiguous conduct and argued that a jury could infer an illegal agreement. The Supreme Court took the case to clarify how courts should evaluate **inferences** at summary judgment — especially when the plaintiff's theory is economically implausible.

Issue

When the non-movant's theory of liability is economically implausible, what level of evidence is required to survive summary judgment?

Holding

To survive summary judgment, the non-movant must produce evidence that **tends to exclude** the possibility of lawful conduct. Ambiguous evidence that is equally consistent with lawful behavior is not enough.

Reasoning

1. **Plausibility Matters.** If the plaintiff's theory is economically irrational, stronger evidence is required to support it.
2. **Competing Inferences.** When the evidence supports both lawful and unlawful explanations, the plaintiff must produce evidence that makes the unlawful explanation **more likely**.
3. **No Jury for Speculation.** Courts must prevent cases from reaching juries when the evidence would require speculation rather than reasonable inference.
4. **Antitrust Context, General Principle.** Although an antitrust case, the Court's reasoning applies broadly: **implausible claims require more persuasive evidence** at summary judgment.

Final Takeaway

Matsushita teaches that **ambiguous evidence is not enough**. When the plaintiff's theory is implausible, they must produce evidence that **rules out lawful explanations**.

DISCOVERY THROUGH CASES

Discovery governs the exchange of information before trial. It is the engine of modern litigation — and the battleground for privilege, work product, and the limits of attorney inquiry.

<u>Attorney–Client Privilege</u> (Simple Explanation)

Attorney–client privilege protects **communications** between a client and their lawyer **made for the purpose of getting legal advice**. It is one of the strongest protections in the law.

Think of it this way:

The client needs a safe space to tell the truth. The privilege creates that space.

What it protects:

- What the client tells the lawyer
- What the lawyer tells the client
- Emails, calls, letters, messages **seeking legal advice**
- Confidential conversations **made for legal guidance**

What it does *not* protect:

- Facts themselves (only the communication about the facts)
- Communications made in public
- Communications not related to legal advice

- Communications made to commit a crime or fraud (crime-fraud exception)

Simple analogy:

Privilege protects the conversation, not the events. If the client says, "I was speeding," the statement is privileged — but the fact that they were speeding is not.

Work-Product Doctrine (Simple Explanation)

The work-product doctrine protects **materials prepared by lawyers (or their team) in anticipation of litigation**. It exists to prevent one side from piggybacking on the other side's strategy.

Two types of work product:

1. Ordinary Work Product

- Notes
- Research
- Chronologies
- Witness lists
- Drafts
- Factual summaries

This can sometimes be discovered if the other side shows a **substantial need** and **cannot get the information elsewhere**.

2. Opinion Work Product

- Mental impressions

- Legal theories
- Strategy
- Evaluations
- What the lawyer thinks is important

This is **almost never discoverable**. Courts treat it as the lawyer's private thought process.

Simple analogy:

Ordinary work product = the lawyer's homework.
Opinion work product = the lawyer's brain.

The rules protect both — but the brain is nearly untouchable.

To Recap:

- **Attorney–client privilege** protects **communications** between lawyer and client.
- **Work-product doctrine** protects **materials and strategy** prepared for litigation.

Privilege = the conversation. Work product = the preparation.

Upjohn Co. v. United States (1981)

Narrative Facts

Upjohn discovered that its foreign subsidiaries had made questionable payments to foreign officials. The company launched an internal investigation led by its general counsel, who sent questionnaires to employees at various levels. The IRS sought the questionnaires and interview notes, arguing that the **attorney-client privilege** applied only to communications with "control group" employees — senior managers who direct corporate decisions. Upjohn refused, asserting privilege and work-product protection. The Supreme Court took the case to clarify the scope of attorney-client privilege in the corporate context.

Issue

Does attorney-client privilege in a corporation apply only to communications with top management, or does it extend to lower-level employees who possess relevant information?

Holding

Attorney-client privilege extends to **all corporate employees** who communicate with counsel at the direction of corporate superiors for the purpose of obtaining legal advice. The work-product doctrine also protects counsel's notes and memoranda.

Reasoning

1. **Rejecting the Control-Group Test.** Limiting privilege to top executives would discourage internal investigations and distort corporate communication.

2. **Functional Approach.** Privilege applies when:

-the communication is made by an employee

-at the direction of corporate superiors

-for the purpose of securing legal advice

-concerning matters within the employee's corporate duties

3. **Work-Product Protection.** Attorney notes, mental impressions, and investigative materials receive heightened protection.
4. **Promoting Compliance.** Broad privilege encourages corporations to investigate wrongdoing and seek legal guidance.

Final Takeaway

Upjohn establishes the **modern corporate attorney-client privilege**: **Privilege protects communications with any employee who provides information needed for legal advice.** It also reinforces strong protection for attorney work product.

Hickman v. Taylor (1947)

Narrative Facts

After a tugboat sank on the Delaware River, killing several crew members, the victims' families sued the tugboat owners. Anticipating litigation, the defendants' attorney interviewed surviving crew members and took detailed notes about their recollections. During discovery, the plaintiffs demanded all written statements and memoranda from those interviews. The defense refused, arguing that these materials reflected the attorney's mental impressions and strategy. The lower courts were divided, and the Supreme Court took the case to determine whether such materials were discoverable under the Federal Rules.

Issue

Are an attorney's interview notes, memoranda, and mental impressions discoverable, or are they protected as attorney work product?

Holding

Attorney interview notes and mental impressions are protected as **work product** and are not discoverable absent a showing of **substantial need** and **undue hardship** in obtaining the information by other means.

Reasoning

1. **Protecting the Adversarial System.** Forcing attorneys to disclose their mental impressions would undermine the integrity of adversarial litigation.

2. **Encouraging Thorough Preparation.** Lawyers must be free to investigate and strategize without

fear that their notes will be turned over to the opposing party.

3. **Qualified, Not Absolute, Protection.** Work product can be discovered only if the requesting party shows:
    - **substantial need** for the materials, and
    - **undue hardship** in obtaining the equivalent information elsewhere.
4. **Witnesses Still Available.** Because the plaintiffs could interview the surviving crew members themselves, they lacked substantial need.

Final Takeaway

Hickman establishes the **work-product doctrine**: **Attorney mental impressions, notes, and investigative materials receive strong protection and are discoverable only in rare circumstances.** This doctrine is now codified in Rule 26(b)(3).

CLAIM PRECLUSION (Res Judicata) THROUGH CASES

Claim Preclusion (also called *res judicata*) prevents parties from relitigating a claim that has already been resolved by a final judgment. Once a court has issued a valid, final decision on the merits, the parties do not get a second chance to bring the same claim or any other claim arising from the same transaction or occurrence.

The core idea is simple: **You get one full and fair opportunity to litigate a claim — not two.**

Claim preclusion promotes finality, efficiency, and fairness by stopping repetitive lawsuits and ensuring that disputes end when the court's judgment becomes final. It applies when three elements are met:

- **Same parties** (or their privies)
- **Final judgment**
- **On the merits**
- **Same claim** (arising from the same transaction or set of facts)

Examples

Example 1: Same Accident, Second Lawsuit (Barred)

A plaintiff sues a defendant for injuries from a car accident and loses after a full trial. The plaintiff cannot file a second lawsuit for additional damages from the **same accident**. The claim has already been resolved.

Example 2: Dismissal With Prejudice (Barred)

A case is dismissed **with prejudice** for failure to prosecute. That dismissal counts as a **final judgment on the merits**, so the plaintiff cannot refile the same claim.

Example 3: New Legal Theory, Same Facts (Barred)

A plaintiff sues for negligence and loses. They later try to sue for strict liability based on the **same event**. Even though the legal theory is different, the claim arises from the same transaction, so it is barred.

Example 4: Different Parties (Not Barred)

A plaintiff sues Defendant A and loses. They later sue Defendant B for the same event. Claim preclusion does not apply because the parties are different (unless privity exists).

Summary

Claim preclusion prevents parties from relitigating the same claim once a court has issued a final judgment on the merits.

Federated Department Stores v. Moitie (1981)

Narrative Facts

Several plaintiffs sued Federated Department Stores for antitrust violations. The district court dismissed the claims. Some plaintiffs appealed; others did not. The non-appealing plaintiffs refiled their claims in state court, hoping for a better outcome. The defendants removed the cases to federal court and moved to dismiss on **res judicata** grounds. The Ninth Circuit tried to rescue the plaintiffs by invoking "public policy" and "simple justice," but the Supreme Court took the case to reaffirm the strictness of claim preclusion.

Issue

Can courts create equitable exceptions to claim preclusion when the result seems unfair?

Holding

No. Claim preclusion is strict. A final judgment on the merits bars relitigation, even if the result seems harsh or inequitable.

Reasoning

1. **Finality Is Paramount.** Once a judgment is final, it binds the parties — even if the judgment is later viewed as incorrect.

2. **No "Simple Justice" Exception.** Courts cannot create ad hoc exceptions based on fairness or sympathy.

3. **Choice Not to Appeal Has Consequences.** Plaintiffs who fail to appeal cannot relitigate the same claim in another forum.

4. **Judicial Efficiency.** Endless relitigation undermines the integrity of the judicial system.

Final Takeaway

Moitie is the hard-edged core of claim preclusion: **A final judgment is final — even if it's wrong, even if it's unfair, even if others in the same case win on appeal.**

Rush v. City of Maple Heights (1958)

Narrative Facts

Rush was injured when she fell from her motorcycle due to a defect in a city-maintained street. She first sued the City of Maple Heights for **property damage** to her motorcycle — and won. Later, she filed a second lawsuit for **personal injuries** arising from the exact same accident. The city argued that she was barred from bringing a second suit because both claims arose from the same event. The Ohio Supreme Court took the case to decide whether a plaintiff can split a single accident into multiple lawsuits seeking different categories of damages.

Issue

Does claim preclusion bar a plaintiff from bringing a second lawsuit for personal injuries after already suing for property damage arising from the same accident?

Holding

Yes. A plaintiff must bring **all claims arising from the same transaction or occurrence** in a single lawsuit. Splitting claims is barred.

Reasoning

1. **One Accident = One Claim.** Even though property damage and personal injury are different harms, they arise from the same underlying event.

2. **Efficiency and Finality.** Allowing multiple suits would waste judicial resources and expose defendants to repeated litigation.

3. **Plaintiff Controls the First Filing.** Because the plaintiff chooses when and where to sue, she must bring all related claims at once.

4. **Modern Transactional Test.** The court embraced the idea that a "claim" includes **all rights to relief arising from the same transaction**, not just the same legal theory.

Final Takeaway

Rush establishes the **transactional test** for claim preclusion: **If two claims arise from the same event, they must be brought together — even if they involve different harms or legal theories.**

Cromwell v. County of Sac (1876)

Narrative Facts

Cromwell held several coupons from municipal bonds issued by Sac County. He sued the county to recover on some of the coupons and **lost** because the court found those particular coupons invalid. Later, he sued again on **different coupons** from the same bond issue. The county argued that the first judgment barred the second lawsuit entirely. The Supreme Court took the case to clarify whether a prior judgment bars only the **same claim** or also bars **different claims** involving similar issues.

Issue

Does a prior judgment bar a later lawsuit involving different claims arising from the same transaction, or does it bar only issues that were actually litigated?

Holding

A prior judgment bars **the same claim** but does **not** bar different claims unless the specific issue was actually litigated and determined in the first case.

Reasoning

1. **Two Doctrines Distinguished.**
    - **Claim Preclusion:** Bars the same claim or cause of action.
    - **Issue Preclusion:** Bars relitigation of issues actually decided.

2. **Different Coupons = Different Claims.** Each coupon was a separate obligation,
-losing on one did not automatically bar suit on another.

3. **Only Issues Actually Litigated Are Precluded.** The first case decided the validity of certain coupons, not all coupons.

4. **Fairness and Precision.** Preclusion must be applied carefully to avoid over-barring claims that were never adjudicated.

Final Takeaway

Cromwell draws the essential line: **Claim preclusion bars the same claim; issue preclusion bars only issues actually litigated and decided.** This case is the conceptual foundation for understanding how the two doctrines diverge.

ISSUE PRECLUSION (COLLATERAL ESTOPPEL)

Issue Preclusion prevents parties from relitigating an **issue** that has already been fully and fairly decided in a prior case. Unlike claim preclusion, which bars entire claims, issue preclusion focuses on **specific questions** that were actually litigated, decided, and essential to the earlier judgment.

The core idea is simple: **If a court has already answered a specific question, the parties don't get to ask it again.**

Issue preclusion promotes consistency, efficiency, and fairness by ensuring that once an issue has been resolved, it stays resolved — even if the second lawsuit involves a different claim or a different legal theory. Courts look for four elements:

- **Same issue**
- **Actually litigated**
- **Actually decided**
- **Necessary to the judgment** Some jurisdictions also require that the party being bound had a **full and fair opportunity** to litigate the issue.

Examples

Example 1: Negligence Decided in Case One (Barred in Case Two)

In a first lawsuit, a court finds that the defendant was **not negligent**. In a second lawsuit involving the same accident, the plaintiff cannot try to relitigate negligence. The issue has already been decided.

Example 2: Different Claim, Same Issue (Barred)

A plaintiff sues for breach of contract and loses because the court finds the contract was **invalid**. The plaintiff later sues for unjust enrichment based on the same agreement. Because the issue of contract validity was already decided, it cannot be relitigated.

Example 3: Issue Not Necessary to Judgment (Not Barred)

A court dismisses a case for lack of jurisdiction but also comments on the merits. Those comments are **not necessary** to the judgment, so they do not have preclusive effect.

Example 4: Issue Not Actually Litigated (Not Barred)

A case ends in a settlement. Because no issues were actually litigated or decided, issue preclusion does not apply.

Summary

Issue preclusion stops parties from relitigating specific issues that were actually litigated, decided, and essential to a prior judgment.

Parklane Hosiery Co. v. Shore (1979)

Narrative Facts

The SEC sued Parklane Hosiery for issuing a false and misleading proxy statement. After a full trial, the court found that Parklane had indeed issued a deceptive statement. Later, private shareholders filed a class action based on the same proxy statement. Instead of relitigating the issue, the shareholders asked the court to apply **offensive non-mutual issue preclusion** — meaning they wanted to use the SEC's victory to bind Parklane, even though the shareholders were not parties to the first case. The Supreme Court took the case to decide whether this type of preclusion is allowed.

Issue

May a plaintiff use a prior judgment offensively to prevent a defendant from relitigating an issue the defendant previously lost against a different party?

Holding

Yes, courts may allow **offensive non-mutual issue preclusion**, but only when it is fair and does not encourage strategic behavior.

Reasoning

1. **Mutuality Not Required.** The Court abandoned the old rule requiring both parties to be bound by the prior judgment.

2. **Fairness Factors.** Courts must consider:

   -Could the plaintiff have joined the earlier action?

-Did the defendant have incentive to litigate fully the first time?

-Are there inconsistent prior judgments?

-Are procedural opportunities different in the second case?

3. **Parklane Had a Full Opportunity.** The SEC case was vigorously litigated, and Parklane had every incentive to defend.

4. **Judicial Efficiency.** Allowing preclusion avoids wasteful relitigation.

Final Takeaway

Parklane authorizes **offensive non-mutual issue preclusion**, but only when fairness supports it. This case modernizes issue preclusion and gives courts discretion to prevent strategic relitigation.

Blonder-Tongue Laboratories v. University of Illinois Foundation (1971)

Narrative Facts

The University of Illinois Foundation owned a patent for a method of manufacturing television antennas. It sued Blonder-Tongue Laboratories for patent infringement. But here's the twist: **another court had already ruled the same patent invalid** in a separate lawsuit against a different defendant. Blonder-Tongue argued that the Foundation should be barred from relitigating the validity of the patent. Under the old rule of **mutuality**, issue preclusion applied only if both parties were bound by the earlier judgment — which wasn't the case here. The Supreme Court took the case to decide whether mutuality should survive.

Issue

May a defendant use **defensive non-mutual issue preclusion** to prevent a plaintiff from relitigating an issue the plaintiff previously lost against a different party?

Holding

Yes. A plaintiff who has fully and fairly litigated an issue — such as patent validity — may be precluded from relitigating that issue against a new defendant. Mutuality is not required.

Reasoning

1. **Fairness to Defendants.** A plaintiff who has already lost on an issue should not get unlimited attempts to relitigate it against new defendants.

2. **Judicial Efficiency.** Courts should not waste resources re-deciding issues that have already been fully litigated.

3. **Full and Fair Opportunity.** Preclusion applies only if the plaintiff had a meaningful chance to litigate the issue the first time.

4. **Ending Mutuality.** The Court rejected the rigid mutuality requirement as outdated and unnecessary.

Final Takeaway

Blonder-Tongue establishes **defensive non-mutual issue preclusion: A plaintiff who loses on an issue cannot relitigate that issue against a new defendant, so long as the first litigation was full and fair.** This case modernizes issue preclusion and aligns it with principles of fairness and efficiency.

Cromwell v. County of Sac (1876)

Narrative Facts

Cromwell owned multiple coupons from municipal bonds issued by Sac County. He sued the county on **some** of the coupons and lost because the court found those particular coupons invalid. Later, he sued again on **different coupons** from the same bond issue. The county argued that the first judgment barred the second lawsuit entirely. The Supreme Court took the case to clarify the difference between barring an entire claim and barring only specific issues that were actually decided.

Issue

Does a prior judgment bar a later lawsuit involving different claims, or does it bar only the **specific issues** that were actually litigated and decided?

Holding

A prior judgment bars only the **same claim**, but it bars relitigation of **issues actually litigated and decided** — even in a different claim.

Reasoning

1. **Two Doctrines, Two Functions.**
    - **Claim Preclusion:** Bars the same claim or cause of action.
    - **Issue Preclusion:** Bars relitigation of issues actually decided, even in a different claim.

2. **Different Coupons = Different Claims.** Each coupon was a separate obligation, losing on one did not automatically bar suit on another.
3. **But Issues Decided Are Binding.** If the first case had decided a general issue (e.g., the entire bond issue was invalid), that issue would carry over.
4. **Precision Matters.** Courts must identify exactly what was decided and apply preclusion only to that.

Final Takeaway

Cromwell is the conceptual foundation of issue preclusion: **Only issues actually litigated and decided are precluded — not everything that could have been raised.** This case draws the bright line between claim preclusion and issue preclusion.

SUPPLEMENTAL JURISDICTION

Supplemental Jurisdiction allows a federal court to hear additional claims that are related to a case already properly in federal court. It prevents parties from having to split their lawsuit between federal and state courts when the claims arise from the same facts, same events, or same dispute.

The key idea is simple: If the claims are so connected that it makes sense to resolve them together, the federal court may hear them.

This authority comes from 28 U.S.C. § 1367 and includes two major parts:

- § 1367(a) — Federal courts *may* hear all claims that form part of the same case or controversy (same nucleus of operative fact).
- § 1367(b) — Limits supplemental jurisdiction in diversity cases to prevent plaintiffs from using extra claims or extra parties to get around the complete diversity requirement.
- § 1367(c) — Courts *may decline* supplemental jurisdiction in certain situations (novel state issues, state claims dominating the case, dismissal of federal claims, etc.).

Examples:

Example 1: Same Case, Same Facts (Allowed)

A car accident happens in Wisconsin.

- The plaintiff sues in federal court under diversity jurisdiction.
- They bring a negligence claim (state law).
- They also add a claim for negligent infliction of emotional distress (also state law).

Both claims come from the same accident, so the federal court can hear both.

Example 2: Federal + State Claim (Allowed)

A plaintiff sues under a federal employment law (federal question). They also add a related state wrongful termination claim.

Because both claims arise from the same employment dispute, the federal court can hear the state claim too.

Example 3: Trying to Add a Non-Diverse Party (Not Allowed in Diversity Cases)

Plaintiff (WI) sues Defendant (IL) in federal court under diversity. Plaintiff wants to add a second defendant who is also from WI.

§ 1367(b) blocks this. Why? Because adding that party would destroy complete diversity, and supplemental jurisdiction cannot be used to get around that rule.

Example 4: Federal Claim Dismissed Early (Court May Decline)

A plaintiff brings a federal claim and a related state claim. The federal claim is dismissed at the start of the case.

The court may choose to dismiss the state claim too, because the federal anchor is gone.

Summary

Supplemental jurisdiction lets federal courts hear related claims that form part of the same dispute — unless doing so would undermine diversity rules or fairness.

Exxon Mobil Corp. v. Allapattah Services (2005)

Narrative Facts

Customers sued Exxon for overcharging at gas stations. Some plaintiffs met the amount-in-controversy requirement for diversity jurisdiction; others did not. The question was whether the federal court could hear the claims of the smaller plaintiffs under **supplemental jurisdiction**. The district court said yes; the Eleventh Circuit said no. The Supreme Court took the case to interpret **28 U.S.C. § 1367**, enacted in 1990 to codify and clarify supplemental jurisdiction.

Issue

When at least one plaintiff in a diversity case satisfies the amount-in-controversy requirement, may the court exercise supplemental jurisdiction over additional plaintiffs who do not?

Holding

Yes. Under § 1367, as long as the court has original jurisdiction over one plaintiff's claim, it may exercise supplemental jurisdiction over related claims of additional plaintiffs — **unless** § 1367(b) expressly forbids it.

Reasoning

1. **Text of § 1367(a).** Grants supplemental jurisdiction over all claims forming part of the same Article III "case or controversy."

2. **§ 1367(b) Limits Only Certain Claims.** The statute restricts supplemental jurisdiction only over

claims by plaintiffs **against** parties joined under Rules 14, 19, 20, or 24 — not claims by additional plaintiffs.

3. **Congress Intended Broad Supplemental Jurisdiction.** The statute was meant to expand, not contract, federal jurisdiction.

4. **Efficiency and Coherence.** Hearing all related claims together promotes judicial economy.

Final Takeaway

Allapattah establishes the modern rule: **If one plaintiff meets the amount-in-controversy requirement, the court may hear the related claims of other plaintiffs — unless § 1367(b) forbids it.**

Owen Equipment & Erection Co. v. Kroger (1978)

Narrative Facts

Kroger, a Nebraska citizen, sued the Omaha Public Power District (OPPD), a Nebraska corporation, in federal court under **diversity jurisdiction**. OPPD then impleaded Owen Equipment under **Rule 14 (third-party practice)**, claiming Owen was responsible for the accident. Owen was believed to be an Iowa corporation, so diversity appeared intact.

During litigation, however, it emerged that Owen's **principal place of business was actually in Nebraska**, making Owen a **non-diverse party**. Kroger then amended her complaint to assert a **direct claim** against Owen — even though she could not have sued Owen directly in federal court at the outset.

The question became: **Can a plaintiff use supplemental jurisdiction to sue a non-diverse third-party defendant brought into the case by the original defendant?**

The Supreme Court took the case to prevent plaintiffs from using joinder rules to circumvent diversity requirements.

Issue

May a plaintiff assert a claim against a non-diverse third-party defendant (joined under Rule 14) using supplemental jurisdiction?

Holding

No. A plaintiff may **not** use supplemental jurisdiction to assert claims against a non-diverse party brought into the case under Rule 14. This would undermine the complete diversity requirement.

Reasoning

1. **Plaintiff Cannot Circumvent Diversity.** The plaintiff controls the initial filing and must respect diversity limits.
2. **Rule 14 Cannot Expand Jurisdiction.** Joinder rules cannot override statutory subject-matter jurisdiction.
3. **Asymmetry Is Intentional.**
    - Defendants may implead non-diverse parties.
    - Plaintiffs may **not** sue those parties unless diversity exists independently.
4. **Fairness and Structure.** Allowing plaintiffs to sue non-diverse third-party defendants would encourage strategic manipulation of joinder rules.

Final Takeaway

Owen Equipment establishes the **core limitation** on supplemental jurisdiction in diversity cases: **A plaintiff cannot use supplemental jurisdiction to sue a non-diverse party joined under Rule 14, 19, 20, or 24.**

Congress later codified this rule in **§ 1367(b)**.

United Mine Workers v. Gibbs (1966)

Narrative Facts

Gibbs was hired to manage a coal-loading operation in Tennessee. When the United Mine Workers union became involved in a labor dispute, violence erupted, and Gibbs lost both his job and a related hauling contract. He sued the union in federal court, asserting:

- a **federal claim** under § 303 of the Labor Management Relations Act, and
- **state-law claims** for interference with contract and other torts.

The question was whether the federal court could hear the **state-law claims** even though they lacked an independent basis for federal jurisdiction. The Supreme Court took the case to define the boundaries of federal judicial power over related state claims.

Issue

When may a federal court hear state-law claims that are related to a federal claim within the same lawsuit?

Holding

A federal court may hear related state-law claims when they arise from a **common nucleus of operative fact** such that the plaintiff would ordinarily be expected to try them all in one proceeding.

Reasoning

1. **Common Nucleus Test.** The state and federal claims must derive from the same set of facts — the same story.
2. **Judicial Economy, Convenience, Fairness.** Supplemental jurisdiction promotes efficient litigation and avoids duplicative lawsuits.
3. **Discretionary Power.** Even when the test is met, courts may decline jurisdiction if:
    - the federal claim is dismissed early,
    - the state issues predominate, or
    - trying them together would confuse the jury.
4. **Federal Claim Must Be Substantial.** The federal claim cannot be frivolous or jurisdictionally defective.

Final Takeaway

Gibbs establishes the foundational rule: **Federal courts may hear state-law claims that share a common nucleus of operative fact with a federal claim, but they retain discretion to decline.**

This test becomes the backbone of **§ 1367(a)** decades later.

JOINDER — THE ARCHITECTURE OF CIVIL LITIGATION

Rule 18 — Joinder of Claims

Rule 18 allows a single party to bring as many claims as they have against an opposing party — whether the claims are related or completely unrelated. Once the parties are properly before the court, the rule is intentionally broad: it lets the plaintiff put every dispute with the defendant on the table at once.

The only real limit is subject matter jurisdiction. Each claim must independently satisfy federal jurisdiction — either through federal question, diversity, or supplemental jurisdiction.

Example

A sues B for breach of contract. **Under Rule 18, A may also add claims for battery, defamation, or conversion — even if they arise from entirely different events — as long as the court has jurisdiction over each claim.**

Summary

Rule 18 permits unlimited claim joinder once the parties are properly before the court, subject only to the boundaries of federal subject matter jurisdiction.

RULE 20 — Permissive Joinder of Parties

Rule 20 allows multiple plaintiffs or defendants to join together in a single lawsuit when their claims arise from the same transaction or occurrence and share at least one common question of law or fact. The rule promotes efficiency and fairness by preventing multiple lawsuits about the same event, but it remains permissive — courts may sever parties if joinder becomes confusing, prejudicial, or unwieldy.

Example

Passengers injured in the same bus crash may join together as plaintiffs against the bus company. Their claims arise from the same event, and they share common questions about negligence, causation, and damages.

Summary

Rule 20 permits multiple parties to join in one action when their claims stem from the same event and share at least one common question.

Narrative Takeaway

Imagine five passengers injured in the same bus crash. They file one lawsuit together. **Rule 20 says: "Yes —** same crash, same questions.**" But if one passenger's claim is based on a completely different incident or theory, the court may sever that claim to keep the litigation manageable and fair.**

RULE 13 — Counterclaims & Crossclaims

Rule 13 — Counterclaims and Crossclaims

Rule 13 governs claims between parties already in the lawsuit. It requires defendants to bring any compulsory counterclaims arising out of the same transaction or occurrence as the plaintiff's claim, or risk losing them forever. It also allows permissive counterclaims (unrelated claims) and crossclaims between co-parties when the claims arise from the same event.

Example

A sues B for breach of contract. If B has a claim against A for unpaid invoices from the same contract, B must bring that counterclaim now — it is compulsory. If B also wants to sue A for a separate loan dispute, that is permissive.

Summary

Rule 13 requires related counterclaims to be brought in the same lawsuit and permits unrelated counterclaims and crossclaims when appropriate.

Narrative Takeaway

Think of Rule 13 as the "don't hold back" rule. If the defendant has a claim tied to the same dispute, they must bring it now or lose it. But if they have unrelated grievances, they can add them too — as long as jurisdiction exists.

RULE 14 — Impleader (Third-Party Practice)

Rule 14 — Impleader (Third-Party Practice)

Rule 14 allows a defending party to bring in a third party who may be liable to them for all or part of the plaintiff's claim. This is about shifting responsibility — indemnity, contribution, or derivative liability. The defendant becomes a **"third-party plaintiff,"** and the new party becomes a **"third-party defendant."**

Example

A sues B for negligence. B believes C is actually responsible and should reimburse B if B loses. Under Rule 14, B may implead C into the lawsuit.

Summary

Rule 14 lets a defendant bring in a third party who may be responsible for paying all or part of the plaintiff's claim.

Narrative Takeaway

Imagine you're sued for a faulty product you sold — but your supplier actually caused the defect. **Rule 14 lets you say, "If I'm on the hook, they're coming in too." It keeps all related responsibility questions in one courtroom.**

RULE 19 — Required Joinder of Parties (Compulsory Joinder)

Rule 19 — Required Joinder of Parties

Rule 19 identifies parties who are so important to the dispute that the case cannot fairly proceed without them. If feasible, they must be joined. If joinder is impossible (e.g., destroys diversity), the court decides whether to dismiss the case or proceed without them.

Example

A sues B over ownership of a piece of property, but C also claims an interest in the same property. C is a required party — the court cannot resolve the dispute fairly without C.

Summary

Rule 19 ensures that essential parties are joined when possible, and guides courts on whether a case can proceed without them when joinder is not feasible.

Narrative Takeaway

Think of Rule 19 as the "we can't decide this without them" rule. If someone's rights will be affected by the judgment, they need to be in the room — or the case may not go forward at all.

RULE 24 — Intervention

Rule 24 — Intervention

Rule 24 allows outsiders to join a lawsuit when they have a strong interest in the outcome. Intervention of right applies when the outsider's interest may be impaired if they are not included. Permissive intervention allows the court to let someone join when their claim shares a common question with the main action.

Example

A lawsuit challenges a state regulation. A business directly affected by that regulation may intervene because the outcome will impact its rights.

Summary

Rule 24 lets outsiders join a lawsuit when they have a significant interest in the outcome or when their participation will aid efficient resolution.

Narrative Takeaway

Rule 24 is the "let me in — this affects me too" rule. When someone's rights or interests are on the line, the rule gives them a doorway into the case, so they're not left out of a decision that shapes their future.

Closing Note

Civil Procedure can be described as the skeleton of the legal system — the structure that holds everything together. But structure alone is not enough. Doctrine becomes meaningful only when it is connected to the people, conflicts, and stories that shaped it. That is the purpose of *Civil Procedure Through Cases*: to bring the doctrine to life through narrative, clarity, and the steady arc of legal evolution.

As you move through these cases — from the modern refinements of *Ford* to the territorial rigidity of *Pennoyer* — you are not just memorizing rules. You are witnessing the transformation of judicial power, fairness, and the reach of the law across time. Each case is a piece of a larger mosaic, and together they reveal how courts balance state authority, individual rights, and the demands of justice.

Thank you for allowing this book to accompany you on your journey. Whether you are a student, or a lifelong learner, may these stories help you see doctrine not as a barrier, but as a bridge — a way to understand how law grows, adapts, and responds to the world around it.

This is only the beginning. More doctrines await. More stories are ready to be told. And the law, in all its complexity, is waiting to be understood — piece by piece.

About the Author

Anjanette G. Seymour is a legal educator, compliance professional, and narrative-driven author dedicated to transforming how law is taught and understood. With an LL.M. from the University of Maryland Francis King Carey School of Law, an LL.B. (Hons.) from the University of London, and certification as a Risk & Compliance Management Professional (CRCMP), she brings both academic depth and real-world experience to her work.

Her career spans legal research, compliance, and authorship, including years of experience in AML/KYC, regulatory interpretation, and cross-jurisdictional compliance. She is also the creator of the **Law in Pieces** series — a growing library of doctrinal books that blend storytelling with legal precision to help readers achieve clarity, confidence, and those rare moments of true epiphany.

Anjanette G. Seymour has authored numerous literary works across genres, and now she's writing narrative legal resources designed to make complex doctrine accessible without sacrificing rigor. Her work is grounded in the belief that law is best learned through stories — stories that illuminate doctrine, reveal purpose, and empower students to think critically and compassionately.

She continues to write, teach, and build resources that honor the heart of legal education: understanding people, understanding conflict, and understanding the principles that guide justice.

REFERENCES & SOURCE MATERIAL

All case summaries in this book are based on publicly available judicial opinions from the United States Supreme Court and federal appellate courts. Judicial opinions are part of the public domain and may be freely summarized, quoted, and adapted for educational purposes.

Primary sources consulted include:

- United States Supreme Court opinions (public domain)
- Federal appellate court opinions (public domain)
- Federal Rules of Civil Procedure (public domain)
- 28 U.S.C. § 1367 and related jurisdictional statutes (public domain)

No proprietary casebook, commercial outline, or copyrighted secondary source was used in the creation of this work.

www.ingramcontent.com/pod-product-compliance
Lightning Source LLC
LaVergne TN
LVHW022225200926
848481LV00006B/2119